RESTORING REASON

RESTORING REASON

*Using the Ancient Liberal Arts to
Defend Against Modern Manipulation*

DR. TRAVIS M. CORCORAN

LIONCREST
PUBLISHING

RESTORING REASON
Using the Ancient Liberal Arts to Defend Against Modern Manipulation

ISBN	978-1-5445-2714-7	*Hardcover*
	978-1-5445-2712-3	*Paperback*
	978-1-5445-2713-0	*Ebook*
	978-1-5445-2715-4	*Audiobook*

George Orwell said, "In a time of universal deceit, telling the truth is a revolutionary act." This book is dedicated to everyone who is courageously seeking and speaking the truth.

CONTENTS

INTRODUCTION

What attracted you to start reading a book about restoring reason?

I'm guessing it's because you have a sense of unease about your life and the world around you. If so, you're not alone. I regularly talk with people who aren't making progress with their business or career, have trouble navigating relationships, can't make confident decisions about their health, and are deeply frustrated with politics.

On an even more basic level, many people are troubled by the thought that they aren't in control of their own lives. Instead of being a self-possessed person of reason who makes good decisions, many fear they're wasting their precious lives trapped in emotional turmoil.

If that describes you, I've got good news and bad news.

The bad news is you're absolutely right to be troubled. That deep sense of unease is because you're being manipulated by big institutions that impact all our lives in toxic ways, and you lack the intellectual tools to defend yourself. If you're feeling personally like you're not in control, it's because you likely aren't. You're letting yourself be dominated by too many differing internal emotional voices.

The good news is that there's a way out. It's not the latest self-help fad. It's not based on the teachings of a charismatic guru, or some recently discovered social science research that will fade away in a few years.

It's grounded in ancient truths about how our minds actually work. It's been around for centuries, and it can restore reason to its proper place in your own life. If enough of us start practicing these ancient arts again, it can also begin to restore reason to our chaotic culture.

Before I tell you about these ancient arts, I want to address some skepticism you may have. I've no doubt you've heard or read claims before that promise they can transform your life for the better, and things didn't turn out as advertised. In some cases, the advice may have even made things worse. Why might this time be different?

For one, most self-help advice these days focuses on the emotions: improving your emotions, managing your emotions, recommendations to force yourself to feel positive emotions. There are a million different spins on the subject, but the fundamental problem is that all these "solutions" preach keeping emotions at the center of your life. This book teaches something radically different. It dethrones emotion and restores reason. Emotion should not be the highest standard you use to judge the quality of your life.

Maybe the thought of giving less power to your emotions and more to reason appeals to you. But that still leaves the question of how to do it. This book offers the answer, which is this: the key to restoring reason is to learn how to practice three ancient liberal arts that together are known as the *trivium*.

Some of you may be aware of this term, while others are thinking, "Triv-vee-what?" Whatever your level of knowledge about the trivium, don't let the unfamiliar name put you off. Properly understood and correctly practiced, nothing is more natural to how the mind works than these three arts.

As a quick bit of background: in traditional learning going back centuries, there are actually seven liberal arts. The trivium refers to the first three and most important of these arts: grammar, logic, and rhetoric. (The other four are mathematics, geometry, music, and astronomy, which aren't relevant to this book's purpose, so we won't cover them.)

Don't let the words grammar, logic, and rhetoric throw you off. Grammar isn't only about where to put commas, logic isn't all that complicated, and rhetoric isn't what politicians use when they want to lie to you in a fancy way.

A helpful way to talk about grammar, logic, and rhetoric is to call them by their ancient names: knowledge, understanding, and wisdom. This is how the ancient Greeks thought about these concepts. Grammar is equivalent to knowledge, logic is the same as understanding, and rhetoric is how you express wisdom.

To put it in even more modern terms, you can see these arts as input, processing, and output. Input is the knowledge in, processing is how you order and understand that input, and output is how you express those results.

We'll use all these terms in this book to refer to the three liberal arts. It's not crucial which labels you use; the point is to understand the underlying concepts.

I also want to explain how I'm using the word reason. As with many important words, reason has a lot of different meanings and senses. For our purposes, reason is a method of thinking and expressing yourself that accords with the arts of the trivium, particularly the second art of logic or understanding.

To clarify even further, restoring reason in your life means you'll stop making impulsive decisions based on whatever emotion is pulsing through you at the moment, and instead become more deliberative and logical in your thoughts and actions.

Grasping these arts and practicing them can dramatically improve the quality of your mind. And once that happens, your life will change for the better. We'll return to this theme at the end of the introduction, but first we have to take a darker detour.

Not Everyone Wants You to Take Back Control of Your Own Mind

There's never been a time in history where taking charge of your own thinking has been easy. No matter what era people lived in, mastering the liberal arts has always taken effort, focus, and commitment.

But it's going to be even harder for you.

That's because you live at a particularly challenging historical moment. We live in an age of cultural chaos and a time dominated by big institutions that don't have your best interests at heart. In fact, they don't want you to succeed in gaining control of your own mind. If you do, they won't be able to easily manipulate you. And if they can't manipulate you, they lose power over you.

The five dominant institutions in our lives are:

- Academia
- Big Corporations
- Big Government
- Big Tech
- Legacy Media

Chapter 1 is all about how much the "Big 5" seep into our lives at the deepest levels, often in ways that we don't fully realize. This theme will thread its way through the entire book because you need to understand what you're up against. If you don't control the quality of your mind, these institutions will be happy to do it. You need to defend yourself against their influence if you want to have any chance of liberating your mind and staying free of their manipulations.

So one way to use this book is as a manual of intellectual self-defense techniques against the relentless efforts of huge institutions to control the culture down to the level of the individual. Knowing and practicing the trivium is an antidote to their poison.

A Quick Guide to Getting the Most Out of This Book

This book is divided into two major sections. The first six chapters start with a brief tour of what you're up against, and then show you how to use the trivium to put logic and reason at the center of your life. By the end of Part 1, you'll understand the basics of each art and how it can help you to think better.

The second section of the book is devoted to understanding more specifically how to put the theory you'll learn into practice. Chapters 6 through 10 of Part 2 will point out how emotion has replaced logic and clear thinking in key areas of our lives: business/career, relationships, health and wellness, and politics.

The last chapter and the conclusion will bring this all together and show you that when you become a person of reason, you'll find people's respect for you naturally grows. You become a successful person of preeminence and influence that others look to for wisdom.

You should also know what this book does not promise. For one, this book will not tell you what to think. I have my own conclusions about specific issues, but one of the points of this book is that you shouldn't let other people or institutions tell you what to think.

This book is not going to tell you things like who to vote for (politics), how to treat a fever (health and wellness), when to sever a friendship (relationships), or specific ways to market your startup (business/career). I will give you some examples and show you pitfalls to watch out for, but I won't tell you what to think. I want to teach you the tools of thinking. What you do with them is up to you.

This book is also not intended to give you a graduate level understanding of the trivium. Its aim is not to be a logic textbook, or to list and explain every technique of rhetoric. My purpose is to give you a solid understanding of what the trivium is, why it matters, and some basics on practicing it in your own life. There are suggestions for further reading at the end of many of the chapters, and I hope you're inspired to keep going.

The Trivium Changed My Own Life

The trivium is not something I knew anything about for the first two decades of my life.

I'm guessing my education was probably a lot like yours. It was compartmentalized, with almost no attempt to connect one subject to another. The central focus was on rewarding the ability to regurgitate knowledge as presented, with little concern about how to evaluate that knowledge. In other words, it was the run-of-the-mill kindergarten through twelfth-grade education that most of us receive.

After high school, I studied nuclear engineering in the US Navy, and later went to a state university, where I earned a degree in philosophy with a minor in biology. My philosophy degree required some basic logic classes, which turned out to be something of a revelation for me.

Up to that point, I considered myself a logical person, as I think most people do. But when I started studying the field of logic in a more systematic way, it was an eye-opener. I wasn't as logical as I thought.

I also discovered that logic is at the heart of philosophy. Logic is to philosophy as mathematics is to science. Whether it's chemistry, biology, or physics, mathematics is crucial to the application and understanding of science. In a similar way, logic, which includes both deductive and inductive reasoning, is crucial to philosophy. Philosophy is unrecognizable if we don't follow the same rules of logic and a chain of reasoning that others can scrutinize.

Understanding the key role logic plays in a life of reason evolved for me into an appreciation of the importance of the other two parts of the trivium. Logic sits at the center, but a full awareness of how to practice it requires a solid grasp of grammar and rhetoric.

When I began to apply the trivium to my own life and decisions, everything improved. I used the trivium to help make decisions in my business, and it skyrocketed. I applied it to my relationships, and they took a turn for the best. I also started thinking about the trivium in relation to decisions about my health. I could analyze what the "experts" were saying with logic and come to my own conclusions. And sure enough, as I close in on the sixth decade of my life, I'm in better health than I was at half my age.

I even started applying it to politics. I'll be honest and say that sometimes that feels like a mixed blessing. When you take emotion and manipulation out of politics and analyze it through the prism of logic and reason, it can be a little depressing to see the shocking lies at the heart of our current politics. Still, I'd rather be clear-eyed and healthy-minded instead of manipulated and not even know it.

The bottom line is that restoring reason with the trivium works. It did for me, and I've witnessed firsthand how it works for others. I've now built a large team around me, and I regularly give workshops on these topics. I'm sought after for mentorship and coaching.

Practicing the trivium leads to real transformation, and it's liberating.

Get Ready to Be Uncomfortable

It's only fair to give you a warning as you proceed. Putting knowledge (grammar), understanding (logic), and wisdom (rhetoric) at the center of your life can get profoundly uncomfortable at times. Cherished beliefs based on childish ideas, cultural programming, or emotional needs must be eliminated if you want to practice these arts with integrity.

As you grow in these arts, you'll also find yourself in opposition to the groupthink of our culture. For example, as you deepen in your understanding, you'll grasp that the frequent refrain that "knowledge is power" is wrong. Power comes from your ability to evaluate the accuracy of knowledge presented to you, and your skill in applying logic to that knowledge. It can sometimes feel easier to float along and let those big institutions tell you what knowledge is.

But if you can push through discomfort and learn to genuinely think for yourself, the rewards are great. Instead of constantly being buffeted by a schizophrenic chorus of conflicting voices centered around emotion, you can listen to the clear and consistent voice of reason.

As you take your journey through this book, remember that it's the quality of your life that is at stake. The chain of reason behind this statement is quite simple:

- The quality of your life will be based on the quality of your decisions, and…
- The quality of your decisions will be based on the quality of your mind, and…
- The quality of your mind is dependent on the proper use of the arts of knowledge, wisdom, and understanding.

In other words, the trivium is the sure path to an increased quality of mind, and therefore a better life.

That's what's on the line. It's an opportunity to transform the quality of your life by restoring reason to the center of your decision-making. But before we tackle how to do it, we need to grapple more fully with the malignant influences of the five formidable institutions that dominate our culture.

Chapter 1

WHY IS OUR CULTURE SO POISONOUS?

There's a well-known saying, originally attributed to business sage Jim Rohn, that says, "We are the average of the five people we spend the most time with." There's some real truth in that expression, but I'd argue that most of us are more influenced by five big institutions than by individuals. Academia, Big Corporations, Legacy Media, Big Tech, and Big Government create the cultural air we breathe and have a fundamental impact on our daily lives. And remember that those five people you spend the most time with are inhaling that same cultural atmosphere, influenced by the same exact institutions that you are.

By influencing us *all* on a daily basis, the impact of these institutions becomes enormous. It's something you'll see clearly if you pause and think about it. Walk through your own day and consider how many touch points you have with these institutions.

The moment you wake up, it's likely to the alarm sound from a smartphone, smart watch, or mass-produced alarm clock. All brought to you by a megacorporation.

Next up is breakfast. Possibly a bowl of cereal produced by a mammoth agricultural/food company like Kellogg's or Unilever, Cargill or Monsanto. Or maybe you stop at a ubiquitous coffee chain that spends millions on marketing to assure you that you'll love their beverages.

While you're consuming breakfast, you turn on a news channel or news radio brought to you by Legacy Media. Impeccably dressed news readers and authoritative voices tell us what's worth talking about, and how to talk about it.

You'll also likely take time in the morning to check your social media feed (Big Tech), or if you're old school, read a major daily newspaper (Legacy Media owned by Big Corporations).

Now it's time to jump in your car, produced by a massive car company. You'll presumably obey all mandated seat belt and traffic laws set by Big Government. If you have children, you may be dropping them off at schools (funded by the government) that teach your children according to whatever educational theories are currently trending in Academia.

There's a good chance that you'll next report to your job at a large corporation—a job you were judged qualified for because you went to college to get Academia's stamp of approval. Whatever your job, there's a good chance you're living in a very insular world, because most of the people around you will have received the same kind of education and obtained that same stamp of approval.

Or maybe you're attending college right now. If so, you'll be under the influence of Academia more directly. You'll discover the path to approval and academic success is the path of least resistance: to think in lockstep with fashionable academic theories that will be handed to you ready-made.

Whether you're in school or at work, you'll need lunch and dinner, and again for most people that will mean meals grown, processed, and packaged by mega corporations. Even if you make an effort to eat organic, non-GMO, or vegan, it's still from some megafarm.

All throughout the day, you're probably checking your social media. Doing lots of Google searches. You're going through your day careful to follow all government regulations and laws. You'll also be catching snippets, or maybe whole stories, from Legacy Media sources as your day progresses.

At night, it's time to relax, and you'll spend your time consuming social media, surfing the internet with algorithms provided to you by Google, and maybe settling in for some entertainment from a huge streaming platform like Netflix.

There really is no escape.

You might be thinking that in some cases you don't want to escape. Perhaps you enjoy your cereal from Kellogg's. You like the idea that the government has set up traffic signals and enforcement for those who fail to obey them. Maybe you loved that movie last night on Netflix.

This book is not going to try to tell you how to think about any of your specific interactions with these institutions. That's for you to think through and decide for yourself. But I do want to point out just how pervasive "Mother Culture" is at this point in human history, and that its all-encompassing presence may not be what is best for human flourishing.

I first read about the idea of Mother Culture in a terrific novel by Daniel Quinn titled *Ishmael*. (I highly recommend it.) One of the key concepts in the novel is that we're born to Mother Nature, but we are raised by Mother Culture. We get our biology from nature, but almost everything else from culture.

To see this more clearly for yourself, go back and again consider your typical day. But this time ask yourself different questions: How many times do you interact with nature on a daily basis? How often did you think of natural processes and how you can align yourself with them? We're so enmeshed in our cultural world that it's hard to come up with touch points with the natural world.

Why does this matter? It's because nature is better input for humans and provides a better blueprint for thinking. Throughout the book we'll talk more about the importance of input (also known as knowledge or grammar in the trivium), but you probably already intuitively grasp that your well-being is better enhanced by a sixty-minute walk in the woods than by an hour of scrolling through Twitter.

Our lives are overwhelmingly artificially constructed, which is already problematic. But it becomes downright poisonous when Mother Culture is controlled by powerful and rich institutions that use emotional manipulation to coerce compliant thinking.

The Big Legacy Institutions Find It More Profitable to Keep You Dependent

Let's go a little deeper and analyze how the big cultural players keep us dependent. Once you start noticing how these institutions foster dependency, you'll be better equipped to identify their influence in your own life.

You'll also have a better grasp of why you need the tools of intellectual self-defense to keep your mind free from their constant encroachment.

Proverbs sometimes get a bad reputation for being bland clichés, but some are quite profound. Here is a proverb directly relevant to this discussion:

"Give a man a fish and you feed him for a day; teach a man to fish and you feed him for a lifetime."

Legacy institutions want you to be dependent on them for all your "fish." They have no interest in teaching you to fish. They want you to eat the fish they produce, and then when you're hungry again, to return to them for more. It's a cycle of dependence that is quite profitable for them but keeps you from living a truly full human life.

Here are some specific examples of how each institution nurtures dependence at the expense of independent thought and action:

Academia

- Instead of encouraging you to think for yourself, Academia is happy to provide you with ready-made sociological and political theories.

- Academia will provide you studies dressed up in scientific language, even when what is presented fails to meet rigorous scientific criteria.

- Academia hopes you don't notice that many of their studies are blatantly contradictory.

Big Corporations

- What consumer goods do you "need" and how can a big corporation make it easier? They are in the business of spoon-feeding you their products and services.

- They pay enormous sums to elite advertising agencies to play on your emotions and keep you buying their products.

- They don't want you to make buying decisions using logic, because then you'll buy less; they prefer emotion and dependence because it's more profitable.

Big Tech

- Big Tech likes to narcotize you by providing a constant stream of social media content that washes over you in a wave of emotion.

- These huge tech companies can arbitrarily cut off certain kinds of content, often with no explanation. (In other words, they'll decide what kind of fish you can have.)

- The most emotional content is usually what goes viral on their platforms. They're not concerned that this further erodes the value of reason in our culture. For them, the formula is simple: more eyeballs = more money.

Legacy Media

- The big Mainstream Media outlets go beyond facts; they'll decide for you the "context" of the facts and present it pre–thought out for you.

- The media will give you a steady diet of infotainment to keep you hooked on entertainment and emotion.

- Media often aid and abet the other big institutions by amplifying their messages, all the while proclaiming themselves to be "fact-checkers" and an "adversarial press."

Big Government

- Entitlements from government only seem to go in one direction: up. This is to keep the "fish" coming in ever-increasing amounts, and to hook as many people as possible on government spending.

- Government prefers you always leave your defense to the police instead of having the tools and training in self-defense.

- Government takes great interest in education; compliant students who are easily manipulated become compliant citizens who are easier to control.

You might object to some of what you just read. You're probably thinking, "Hey, I like some of the 'fish' provided by these institutions." To pick some random examples, you might enjoy being able to go to the grocery store and purchase a jar of spaghetti sauce instead of growing your own tomatoes. Or you like the option to call the police instead of defending yourself. And you want to be able to take advantage of academic resources and knowledge produced by others.

Those are fair points, so let's return to our original proverb and extend it a bit and say this: taking a fish that is given to you is not the problem. The problem is this: What if your "benefactor" stops providing you fish? Or what if they keep lowering the quality of the fish they provide? Then you're stuck wallowing in dependence.

The crucial concept is that the more you can become self-sufficient (teach yourself to fish), the more control you have over your own life. Then you can choose what fish you want to accept, and what fish you want to catch for yourself.

I'm not teaching that you should never shop at a grocery store, or never call the police, or ignore everything that academics produce. My counsel is to learn the arts that allow you to analyze your choices with reason and logic. When you improve your mind's quality, then you'll be able to separate mindless, emotional dependence from the free choice to accept what's offered.

Knowledge Is Not Power

There's a false concept that makes it easier for institutions to mislead us, and that's the oft-heard phrase, "Knowledge is power," as I mentioned in the introduction.

It sounds good. But it's not true.

Properly defined, knowledge is simply a statement about reality. Absorbing knowledge is easy, which is why it's not power. (Nothing easily gained gives you real power).

Here's some examples of knowledge statements, selected completely at random:

- Water is a molecule made up of two parts water, and one part oxygen.
- My shirt is red.
- Diamond cuts glass.
- All humans are mortal.

Anyone of normal intelligence can imbibe an arbitrary collection of facts.

I don't want to give you the idea that knowledge isn't important. It is, and the trivium can't work without accurate knowledge as the first step. But for knowledge to become useful and give you power, you need to apply logic to it. We'll dive deeper into this as the book progresses, but for now all you need to grasp is that knowledge is not the same thing as a conclusion drawn from that knowledge.

Institutions do this all the time; they tell you what your conclusion should be, but label it as knowledge. This is how the talking head on television can confidently assert he's "reporting the facts" but fail to acknowledge all the assumptions and logical missteps he's made on the way to the "knowledge" he's presenting. (Sadly, I believe some of these institutional messengers don't even realize what they're doing.)

You should get as much of your knowledge as possible from direct experience. If it doesn't grow out of your own experience, you're getting it from culture. But what if that culture is not healthy, and that well of knowledge is poisoned?

This false idea that knowledge is power has some accomplices. Let me give you an example of what I mean.

In our culture, literacy is celebrated and put on a pedestal. Don't get me wrong, I'm not anti literacy. Literacy is necessary, and you can't fully practice the trivium without it. But it should be considered the first baby step toward a life of reason, not celebrated in and of itself. It's analogous to the falsehood that knowledge is power.

Let's walk through how you become literate to understand better what I'm driving at.

Your first step toward literacy starts with hearing language, primarily through your parents in the beginning. You start connecting the word "mom" with this person, and "dad" with that person. You identify "cat" with that furry thing, and "banana" with those funny-shaped yellow objects you like to eat. In other words, you're gaining knowledge, but your brain hasn't matured enough to understand how to process that knowledge into rational conclusions.

That's why parents are constantly using language about what's right and wrong, and what actions are safe and unsafe. They're doing the processing and logic for their children and telling them what the conclusion should be. This is totally appropriate for children until they reach the age of reason (usually around age seven or eight).

During this first stage, you begin to make the transition to reading and writing. But even with this new way of consuming language, you aren't truly understanding it. You're still simply collecting all this language data and gathering knowledge through mimicry and memorization.

And reading is an amazing skill. If we simply celebrated literacy as a wonder of early childhood, that would be fine. But instead, it becomes the pattern for the rest of our journey through typical educational institutions. The focus stays almost exclusively on taking in knowledge, and there's relatively little interest in teaching you the tools to evaluate that knowledge. (We'll talk about this more later, but why do almost no high schools offer courses in basic logic? It's equivalent in importance to teaching mathematics, but somehow we don't.)

In the end, literacy is simply an effective conduit for inputting data into a human mind. And that data you're absorbing through literacy could be accurate, or not. Even if the knowledge is accurate, it has little value if you don't know how to evaluate it and come to truthful conclusions.

Seen in this light, literacy is a neutral skill, a tool, not something to be worshipped for itself. So even though our culture presents literacy as something to be proud of, it's more like holding a hammer. Everything depends on how you're going to use that hammer. Will you be building a house, or will you be swinging it to smash all the windows in the house?

I believe the idea of literacy as a great good in itself is a holdover from history when only wealthy aristocrats could read and write. It's a great historical achievement that literacy is much more widespread in most modern cultures.

But this worship of literacy blinds us to the fact that many times all we're reading is propaganda produced by a toxic culture that discourages thinking independently about that knowledge. In this way, the hammer of literacy is used as a tool to pound us into mental bondage.

If too many people can't think for themselves and simply parrot what they learn, the cultural environment becomes toxic. In this way, literacy can be even worse than illiteracy if it's used to fill you with false ideas. Without understanding how to reason we can only shout at each other in emotional outrage.

The question becomes, how do you heal from this? How can you start cultivating and nurturing a better quality of mind? How can you begin to evaluate knowledge, and judge what has value and what doesn't? If you can't do this for yourself, you're left trapped, having to always take conclusions on the faith of authorities, or being guided only by your feelings.

There are many self-help gurus who say they have an answer to these problems. Let's see if they can help us.

Chapter 2

WHY TYPICAL SELF-HELP ADVICE MAKES THINGS WORSE

Faced with feelings of discomfort and a sense of anxiety, we want to do something about it. That's the natural human desire, to make the uneasiness and unhappiness go away.

It's understandable that people would turn to those who share self-help advice or even to a New Age spiritual advisor. People are hurting, and these folks say they have a solution. A huge part of the problems in our culture is rooted in letting our emotions be manipulated.

So what antidote do these experts come up with? In many cases, what they counsel is more manipulation of your emotions, but this time they want you to do the manipulating yourself. Basically, most of the advice boils down to denying all or part of reality in order to soothe and gratify our emotions.

I say this because much of the self-help section of the bookstore is dedicated to denying unpleasant parts of reality. And even worse than the self-help movement is what is typically referred to as New Age spirituality.

What most of this advice has in common is to favor indulging your emotions instead of a reasoned engagement with reality.

I want to be clear that emotions are not the enemy. You should not try to pit your reason against emotion, as if one needs to be eliminated for the other to function properly. Each has a role to play. I'll go more in depth in the next chapter on the appropriate role of emotions. For now it's enough to say that you should not sacrifice a commitment to truth just to soothe your emotions.

This reliance on emotion is exactly why most self-help advice and all New Age ideals fail. Emotions don't work as a solution, because they're fleeting. That's integral to their function; they're meant to change because emotions are real-time feedback. If you find yourself in a threatening environment, you should feel fear. If you find yourself in a loving environment, you should feel content.

But the fleetingness of emotions is also why they should not be the basis for decisions. Good decisions rely on gathering knowledge and applying logic to what you collected. That's a repeatable, reliable process for making high-quality decisions, and something on which you can build a high-quality life.

Let's get a little more specific about the typical guidance you hear from seeming experts and self-styled gurus and analyze what's wrong with it. I've put together a list of fifteen different kinds of advice that we've all heard at one time or another.

1. Ignore the Negative, Focus on the Positive

This won't work because it counsels ignoring some parts of objective reality. It can be harsh to accept sometimes, but we know life is full of both challenges and opportunities, and of things both bad and good. To say you're only going to focus on one side is to commit yourself to willfully ignoring the negative parts of reality.

As we'll see in the next chapter, practicing the trivium is about a commitment to truth and objective reality. To ignore it invites problems, because you're grounding your life in an illusion.

The self-help gurus who preach this want you to feel good while you're around them, or watching their videos, or reading their books. But when the truly negative happens, you awake to the fact that you were trying to live on delusional advice.

2. Never Get Angry

This won't work because it's unnatural. Anger is an emotion, and we're equipped with it for a reason.

To give an extreme example: If I walk up and strike you unprovoked and you refuse to get angry, I'm going to think there's something wrong with you. Anger serves a purpose, just like fear does. The key is learning to distinguish irrational angers from rational angers.

There's a good analogy with fear. Fear as an emotion may save your life. It's what keeps prey alive and tells it to run from a predator.

In the same way, anger can be a good indicator that something is wrong and unjust. It motivates people to take action and right wrongs. To pledge to never get angry is to shut off part of your humanity and to deny an important emotion. And it's always a bad idea to deny part of yourself.

This idea that we should meditate away all anger is foolhardy. The correct approach is to ask if the anger is justified. And if it is, then what is the appropriate action?

This is the proper way to use an emotion as an initial gauge of a situation. Then we take a step back and use reason to analyze the accuracy of the emotion.

3. All Is Good, Evil Is an Illusion

Most people instinctively realize this is an absurd statement, but you'd be surprised how many New Age "prophets" preach this. Even people who sense how inaccurate it is can, in weak moments, start to slide toward affirming it.

No matter how wise a voice someone uses for this kind of pronouncement, it's still moral relativism, and it's another way to dodge the reality of the world.

A few simple examples destroy this argument. If we affirm evil as an illusion, what basis would we use to condemn Adolf Hitler and the Nazi regime?

On a more personal level, if someone robs, assaults, or murders a loved one, are you prepared to say there is no evil and that all is good? No matter how many times you chant all is good, there is still good and evil, and we are not beyond it.

4. *Everything Is Subjective, So Every Individual Can Decide What They Think Is True*

To say this is to essentially assert that no real knowledge is possible. This idea ends in nihilism and futility because it eliminates any chance of agreeing upon objective truths and definitions with other people. It would be like trying to play a sport without a shared set of rules.

In my experience, this philosophy is one of the more popular evasions of reality, and people like it for two main reasons:

The first reason has some good intentions behind it: we don't want to attack people or be coercive in imposing our views on someone. But defending the truth is too important to take this cop-out.

The second reason is less understandable: claiming that "everything is subjective" appeals to people because it justifies intellectual laziness. Pursuing objective truth requires intellectual rigor, and at times discomfort, because it may force you to give up cherished beliefs.

However, some intellectual discomfort is not a good enough reason to descend into solipsism. If there's no objective truth, there's no way we can really talk productively with others about things that matter. We're all trapped in a universe of one.

I want you to notice something else about this erroneous world view. For self-help gurus, promoting relativism gives them license to say pretty much whatever they want, even things that are nebulous and ambiguous, or have no meaning at all. If everything is subjective, they can never be wrong.

5. All Is an Illusion

This is a combination of the ideas embedded in the previous two examples. It's solipsism dressed up in a mystical-sounding formula. If the visible universe is all an illusion, we can't have any meaningful knowledge about it.

It's also impossible to call someone to account for their actions if everything is an illusion.

6. Evil Has to Exist to Balance the Good

You'll sometimes hear this from New Age types, but also from people with advanced psychology degrees. They claim that without evil there can be no good, and that evil is the shadow side, there to balance out the good and create an integrated whole.

The truth is that evil is not necessary, it's just available as a moral choice. But the potential for something doesn't mean it must occur. There's absolutely no evidence that the dark side needs to balance the light.

Would we want to say that the atrocities of history had to happen in order for good to exist? I don't think that's a position you'd want to have to defend.

7. Accept Everything, Resist Nothing

Underpinning this idea is a fatalism that says our destiny has already been decided for us. This has the attraction of taking the responsibility out of our hands. Theoretically, it would eliminate all the anxiety and stress of making our own decisions and holding ourselves accountable for those choices.

It says that if we can simply accept everything that happens to us, we no longer will have any true worries. The lie behind this is easily exposed. If a woman is being sexually assaulted, she should just not resist? We do resist things, and we should.

There's another formulation of this philosophy that is often stated as "Everything happens for a reason." That's a true statement. But the problem is that most people who say it want to stop there. They aren't interested in analyzing what those actual reasons are. That is an escape from reality.

The proper response is, "Yes, everything does indeed happen for a reason, and let's discuss what those reasons are." This then can become a way to explore and better understand reality instead of hiding from it.

8. The Law of Attraction

This is the belief that your thoughts can attract material things to you. In other words, think that you'll get something—wealth, specific goods, whatever—and that thought will cause it to happen.

The obvious error is supposing that thoughts can attract things. It's only real-world actions that can create wealth and produce goods. In business, if you provide a good service or product, then you get something of value in return. That's an action that produces things.

The idea behind the law of attraction actually has an echo of truth. The whole point of this book is that if you can improve your quality of mind, your quality of life will improve. But that happens because you're making better decisions, leading to better actions.

The gurus peddling the idea of the law of attraction skip the discipline of doing the work. They turn the use of the mind toward the childish idea of wish fulfillment.

9. Don't Blame or Judge Others

The idea here is that having negative feelings towards others will rebound on you, leading to negativity in your own life. While avoiding overly harsh judgments is fine, we also need to acknowledge that people do bad things and are morally culpable for those actions. That's just an objective fact.

People need to take 100 percent responsibility for their actions. Giving people license to deny responsibility and blame or excuse bad behavior on environmental factors, history, or socioeconomics is detrimental to both the individual and society.

This idea of never judging is hugely popular with New Age proponents because they claim that blame and judgment are always negative and that forgiveness is an unqualified positive. Which leads us to number ten.

10. Forgive No Matter What

This is a false idea of forgiveness. If someone has not sincerely apologized for a wrong action, has zero regrets, and has made no effort to change, why would you forgive them? Some people answer that they do it for their own peace.

But true peace is rooted in honesty, and forgiving indiscriminately is a dishonest act. Holding people to account for their actions is honoring truth and reality.

11. We Should Fear Chaos Above All

Order is good, but it's not the only good. Some self-help experts exploit the fear of chaos to the point that they counsel order above all. Some politicians also use this fear to justify authoritarian laws and regulations.

Creativity is born out of chaos and we shouldn't have an undue fear of it. A certain amount of chaos is the price of freedom. We fear external chaos too much and don't fear internal chaos enough. What should truly frighten us is internal chaos in our own minds. (The trivium is an excellent way to tame the chaos of our minds).

The fear of external chaos makes us accept too many limitations on our freedom, while our internal chaos allows us to be manipulated. A comparison of our cultural world with the natural world is illuminating. In nature, the whole world is anarchy. Animals, birds, and plants are all free to do as they please.

We humans have the internal and external reversed when compared to the rest of nature. Most of us allow internal anarchy to hold sway in our minds, allowing multiple voices of emotion to rule us from one minute to the next. Meanwhile, our external world is ruled oppressively by the government, which creates ever-tightening rules regulating our behavior.

The goal should be the opposite. You should govern yourself internally as a monarchy, with the single voice of reason on the throne. Our external world should be in accordance with the rest of nature, without government oppression and without a fear of anarchy. Etymologically, the word anarchy simply means "without a ruler." Anarchy is not about disorder; it's about freedom.

12. Defending Truth Is Not Worth Doing Because It Creates Conflict

This instruction has an advantage over most of the guidance on this list because it at least admits that truth exists. However, peace at the cost of truth is not a good trade. If we don't defend truth, and do it vigorously, then we are tacitly conceding that truth really doesn't matter very much.

A failure to stand up for truth also cheats people who could benefit from it and desperately need to learn it. By refusing to defend it out of fear of conflict, you're stealing an opportunity from others.

13. Enlightenment Means Feeling Good All the Time

There are some who encourage a version of "enlightenment" that is portrayed as unending bliss, harmony, and peaceful meditation. Follow their advice, and they claim you'll become enlightened.

That's not true enlightenment. When you flip a light switch on in a room and it goes from dark to light, you're going to see everything more clearly. That's going to include the cobwebs in the upper corner of the ceiling, the dirt on the carpet, and the bug crawling out from under the sofa.

And that's the real purpose of enlightenment: to see more clearly. Don't fall for a definition of enlightenment based on a phony sense of feeling good. Commit to enlightening yourself about reality and seeing everything. If your goal is to only feel good, you'd do better to keep the light switch off.

14. Love Is All You Need

Love is a great thing, and it's important in a well-rounded life. One problem with the word love, however, is that it's often vaguely defined. This means that when someone gives this advice, people fill in their own conception of what they mean by love.

But even when properly defined, love is still not all you need. Love doesn't pay the rent or put food on the table. Love is a wonderful thing, but it's only one of a full spectrum of emotions. Love has a role just like all of them do, but it's only a part of life, not everything you need.

15. A Savior Will Come

The desire for a savior is a long-standing human temptation that many gurus exploit. They'll seduce people by talking like this: "Things are going to happen at the right time and right place. The universe will coalesce, and things will unfold to reveal everything was necessary to prepare for the next stage of humanity. Trust the universe because the great awakening is almost here."

With the inevitable anxieties and stresses of life, people feel relieved when someone tells them all troubles will disappear soon. There's no need to be responsible for your own future, because someone or something is coming.

The version I just outlined is extreme (although some gurus do talk like that). But beware also of more subtle versions that play on the idea of "the end of your problems is just around the corner and it's all going to be easy after that."

Taking responsibility for your own future and your own

intellectual growth is challenging, but it's better than waiting for a savior.

Those are fifteen false ideas to watch out for, and they all share the idea of denying some part of reality or yourself in order to feel better temporarily. Many of these "solutions" have the extra advantage of loopholes that allow the advice giver to escape accountability when their guidance fails.

There's one other unfortunate idea in our culture that gets expressed with regularity and I think it's important to address it. It's closely related to number four on the list ("Everything Is Subjective…") but it's expressed in a particularly pernicious form. That's any statement where a possessive pronoun is coupled with the word truth.

People are now encouraged and told, "Hey, just speak your truth." Others will say things like, "This is my truth." When you hear any talk about "my truth" or "your truth," it's a sure indication that the speaker doesn't understand the meaning of the word.

Truth is an objective concept. You may have your perspective or your ideas or your beliefs or your feelings, but there's no such thing as your truth or my truth or her truth or his truth. Truth is a factually principled statement that conforms to reason and evidence and doesn't change based on our feelings. That's not what people mean when they say "my truth" and "your truth."

What they're really saying is, "This is how I feel right now." Tomorrow their truth may change. But that's not truth then. To say, "My truth versus your truth" is as absurd as if someone said, "My gravity versus your gravity." It's just gravity, period.

What Should We Do?

If we can't trust our institutions because they have a vested interest in manipulating us, and if the typical self-help and New Age spirituality offers us false cures, what do we do?

We start by understanding that there's a clear distinction between thinking and feeling (between reason and emotion). Most self-help advice revolves around manipulating your feelings and overriding thinking. We're about to go in a better direction, one that is rooted in the proven arts of the trivium.

We won't be completely ignoring emotions and feelings, but we also won't be letting them rule us.

Chapter 3

TRAINING YOUR MIND USING THE ANCIENT ARTS OF THE TRIVIUM

To get control of your mind, you need two things: an understanding of how it works, and then a method for disciplining your mind to produce thought that's truthful and accords with reality.

Happily, the trivium provides both. It gives you an understanding of how the mind works because it aligns with the mind's development and function. Instead of the artificially imposed cultural ideas that undergird most education today, these traditional arts work because they match the natural functioning of the human mind.

The trivium also provides a practical tool kit for reasoning itself, and for producing thought outcomes that you can trust and that lead to better quality decision-making.

These arts have ancient roots, and there's a reason why they've never completely disappeared. You can't completely suppress something so naturally human. Since the term trivium may be new to many of you, or only vaguely understood, the goal of this chapter is to give you a broad overview so you can see its value.

First, don't think of the trivium as something esoteric or requiring some special talents. The traditional terms for these arts—grammar, logic, and rhetoric—give some people the idea that this is highly complex. While it's true you can continue to deepen your understanding of these arts and it can get more technical, this book is an introduction to the basics.

If you struggle with the traditional terms, remember we can also call these arts knowledge, understanding, and wisdom, or input, processing, and output.

A good way to understand the beautiful simplicity of these concepts is to see how they match up to the developing human mind. These arts are a natural fit to the mind's growth and functioning.

Think about a child up to about age seven. During that time, a child's mind is essentially a sponge, soaking up knowledge. Children identify things like mommy, daddy, cup, cereal, fire truck, and everything else in the world. Young children also identify some abstract and immaterial concepts like "I'm hungry" and "I feel hot."

In this early stage, words are being linked to things and to concepts. The child is developing a database that will be used and added to throughout his or her entire life span. Data is being collected by the mind, but there's not much logical processing going on.

Then around the age of seven (it can start earlier or later, but seven is somewhat typical), there's a shift. This is when the thirst for understanding begins. This is the age when the child's internal processor starts developing, and questions of logic become more urgent. This is why kids around this age begin questioning concepts like Santa Claus.

Once the amount of data reaches a certain quantity and the mind is developed enough, humans transition away from accepting all data at face value, and the mind starts asking questions about it. How does a large roly-poly man travel to every single house in the world in one night? How does he come down a chimney? How do reindeers fly?

Data gets compared with other data in the mind. The child has never seen a dog or horse fly. Does it seem likely that reindeer fly? The database has become significant enough for evaluation and comparison to occur, and logic becomes the next natural step in the development of the human mind.

Of course, seven-year-olds won't be walking around talking in syllogisms just yet. The processing power of logic starts developing slowly, and meanwhile the knowledge database continues to expand, too. Once both have progressed enough, the third phase of mental development begins. This typically happens in a person's early teens. This is when young men and women begin to express wisdom based on knowledge and understanding. (Or, to update the terms a bit, the teen uses his knowledge data input, runs it through his mind processor, and begins producing output.)

This is why the term sophomore is used for American high school students around this age, because etymologically that word means "wise fool." The students are just beginning to develop the skills of rhetoric/output/expression, and so likely will sound like wise fools as they stumble towards mastery of this art.

The larger point to grasp among these details is that these three liberal arts align with the natural and organic development of the human mind.

Of course, this outline of the development of the human mind is not meant to imply that each of these phases is complete as you reach the next stage. You'll continue adding to your stock of knowledge throughout your lifetime; your grasp of logical principles and comparing data should sharpen over time, if you put in the effort; and you'll get better at expressing your output (wisdom/rhetoric).

Even though you should keep developing these skills naturally throughout your lifetime, we'd all be a lot better off if our educational institutions and our culture supported these natural stages and looked for ways to strengthen them. Unfortunately, that's not what happens in our government-run schools, nor in most private schools, and not even in colleges and universities, at least not with any consistency. For many people, this means that these arts atrophy and become weaker, instead of naturally stronger.

When you stop and think about it, philosophy courses are virtually nonexistent in high school, including logic. It should astonish us that you can graduate high school without ever being taught basic logical thinking. Logic is so basic to quality thinking, and yet we don't teach it in schools. You can even get a higher education degree and never be taught basic logic!

Unfortunately, the problem is even larger than the absence of teaching the art of logic. It's also the methods and behavior that gets rewarded in our schools.

Everything is rigidly compartmentalized: During this hour, you're going to learn math. Bell rings. During the next hour you're going to learn history. Bell rings. Now you'll learn science. For each time period, you are lectured to while sitting in neat rows. It's reminiscent of Pavlov's dogs, right down to the ringing of the bells.

What it doesn't do is teach students to take knowledge, develop it logically, and thoughtfully integrate subject matter. Instead, the mentality is, "What do I need to know to ace this specific math test? How can I learn the right words to do well on the vocabulary section of the college or university entrance exam?"

These are the common mindsets that our educational approach instills in even the best students. In fact, the students with the highest marks are the ones who learn that the winners in this system are those who can regurgitate the answers as closely as possible to how they were packaged.

For the most part, the idea of giving you the tools of analysis to think for yourself are either never brought up or not emphasized. The experts who wrote the textbooks will feed you the conclusions you need.

What this shows us is that our schools stop after the first liberal art: knowledge. Recall our discussion of knowledge and literacy in Chapter 1. We are being given prepackaged facts, but not taught to:

1. Analyze whether the knowledge is an accurate reflection of reality.
2. Asked to work with that knowledge in a logical way so we could truly learn how to think for ourselves.

What's missing is the middle step. If we were talking about computers, it would be like the processor had been removed. Our education is all input and output. They input, you memorize and give them back the output, which matches the input to the letter—at least if you want high marks.

I realize there are private schools here and there that do teach quality thinking skills, but that's truly rare and exceptional. And, of course, you can sometimes be fortunate to have a teacher, mentor, or coach who teaches you how to think (most times they won't call it the trivium, but they are teaching you in accordance with its principles). Or maybe like me you study philosophy in college and are required to take a basic logic course that opens your eyes. Unfortunately, all these circumstances are the exceptions.

We need to remember the cost of this poor education. When you're simply taught to regurgitate input, you become intellectually defenseless, which leaves you easy prey for emotional manipulators. Our schools prepare us well for "experts" and big institutions to hand us our thoughts, all the while using emotion to make us feel like what they say is true.

The Trivium Has Ancient Roots

This book is not a history of the trivium, but its ancient roots are worth noting. The natural operations of the mind have been studied and known since the ancient world of the Greeks and Romans. The thinkers of those civilizations applied their own minds to the study of how the mind thinks, and it revealed to them the arts they called knowledge, understanding, and wisdom.

In the Middle Ages and Renaissance, academies came into being and scholars further refined these concepts and called them grammar, logic, and rhetoric. The methods and ideas were developed more formally during this time, but the underlying idea of how the mind worked remained the same.

The long history of these arts demonstrates that they are a trusted and proven way to a higher quality of mind. It also adds weight to the idea that these arts truly reflect how the mind naturally works, as has been confirmed through centuries of use. You're being handed a gift with deep roots.

Committing to the Trivium

The next three chapters will go over each art of the trivium in more detail, but there's something you need to know before we go into this deeper. For the trivium to impact your life, you need to genuinely commit to learning and practicing these arts.

Let's face it. It's easier in the short run to give in to emotional manipulation and not do the rigorous intellectual work required to restore reason in your life. In the long run, there's a cost, of course. But just like skipping workouts, it sometimes feels better to forgo long-term benefits for short-term laziness.

What will help you commit, and then stay committed? In my experience, three things keep people focused and doing the work.

First, they recognize the value of the trivium. That's why a big part of this book's mission is to demonstrate that learning the trivium has immense worth for improving the quality of your mind.

Second, you need to build on that recognition and nurture a desire for practicing these arts in your daily life. How many things in life do we know are good for us but we don't take the actions we need to? People who transform their lives through reason cultivate a desire for the goods of the trivium. Remind yourself what's at stake in your own life. Try it out and see the difference it makes. Compare it to times you react emotionally. Which one improves your life: responding with reason or reacting with emotion? This is the kind of reflection you should do on a regular basis.

Finally, you need to have a strong self-image or work on developing one. I find that people who value themselves also value ways to strengthen the quality of their lives. The good news is that the more you improve the quality of your mind, the more it will reinforce a strong self-image. If you struggle with a weak self-image, ask yourself why. Some reflection can often point to the fact that you're letting other people dictate how you see yourself.

And don't forget that there's no substitute for taking action. Action will breed more confidence and a stronger self-image.

I can't emphasize enough that the trivium takes commitment, and you must be willing to take responsibility for your own mind. If you can bring a recognition of the value of the trivium, a desire for its benefits, and a strong self-image, you'll get there. If you aren't willing to commit, the trivium is not going to work for you.

In addition to commitment, there are four core values that are particularly desirable for a successful pursuit of the classical liberal arts. If these values are already deeply embedded in your character, it will be a significant help on your journey. If you have only a lukewarm commitment to these values, reflect on why. The more you make your life revolve around these values, the stronger you'll become.

Core Value: Freedom (Liberty)

This is a deep belief in the power of choice and freedom from restraint. That this core value meshes with these arts is evident when you consider that "liber" is the root term for both liberty and liberal arts. Those who place the highest importance on making their own choices insist on doing it without the influence of nefarious deception, manipulation, or coercion. If you don't have intellectual liberty, you will also lose physical liberty.

As the revolutionary Mikhail Bakunin said, "The liberty of man consists solely in this, that he obeys the laws of nature, because he has himself recognized them as such, and not because they have been imposed upon him externally by any foreign will whatsoever, human or divine, collective or individual."

Core Value: Integrity

This is the state of being whole and undivided. It's important to anyone who desires being whole or complete that they do not neglect their intellectual capacity, to go along with their physical and emotional capacity. While emotional and physical health are certainly important to wholeness, one is incomplete without intellectual health.

According to the eighteenth-century writer Samuel Johnson, "Integrity without knowledge is weak and useless, and knowledge without integrity is dangerous and dreadful."

Core Value: Congruence

This is the quality or state of agreeing, coinciding, or being congruent with your own internal thought processes and your output to the world. Some people don't seem to mind being contradictory and inconsistent, but internal conflict has a price, leading to stress in the individual whose thoughts, speech, and behavior do not agree or coincide. Additionally, people who do not value congruence often lose the respect of others, negatively impacting their personal and professional efforts at preeminence.

The Jainist called Mahavira agrees: "By sincerity, a man gains physical, mental and linguistic straightforwardness, and harmonious tendency; that is, congruence of speech and action."

Core Value: Responsibility

This is a commitment to be accountable to yourself and others. The quality and condition of an individual's life is the sum of external circumstances plus the response or reaction of the individual. When one chooses emotional reaction over reasoned response, that person lives at the mercy of those who induce emotional reactions. Take responsibility for how you respond or you will never be free.

Author and speaker Jim Rohn has said, "You must take personal responsibility. You cannot change the circumstances, the seasons, or the wind, but you can change yourself."

What about Emotions?

I stated earlier that emotions are not our enemy, and we shouldn't view emotion as the opposition to reason. Yet, at the same time, I've also emphasized that letting emotions drive our reactions causes us big problems.

What exactly is the role of emotions? Before we go deeper into the trivium, it's time to meet this issue head-on.

The purpose of emotions is not to be the basis for decision-making, nor a consistent way to draw conclusions. They are simply indicators, sometimes reliable, of our current feelings toward any situation.

Yet what about extreme situations? For instance, if a vicious dog is charging at you, the emotion of fear is excellent feedback. In these types of intense situations requiring immediate reactions, emotions are especially valuable.

But extremes are by definition rare, so we can't base much on them. When we move out of the realm of the extreme, things get trickier. In your everyday life, you'll experience a range of emotions as the flow of your circumstances changes. There's a tendency to continue to use emotion as the basis for reactions, just like you would in a more extreme moment of danger. But in normal circumstances, that's a mistake.

Emotions are feedback, and except in life-threatening situations, it's better to analyze that feedback for accuracy. In other words, never use emotions to react except in the severest situations. Instead, pause. Then use reason to respond, using the emotions you feel as one piece of feedback.

Another way to think of this is in terms of what voices you're going to listen to. When it comes to emotions, the voices are multiple, variable, and constantly shifting. The voice of reason is singular. If you're using the basic outline of the trivium, it will guide you to quality decisions rooted in one logical voice. Which do you think will lead to better quality decisions and actions in your life—the multiple, chaotic, ever-changing voices of emotion, or the one stable voice of reason?

Think of emotions like the warning lights on your car dashboard. Your check engine light comes on. That could be a false alarm due to a malfunctioning light or a faulty sensor. Or it could be a serious problem. It's not something to overreact to; it's something to have investigated for the proper response. And all the while, you want reason to be the steady hand on the steering wheel.

There's one more aspect to all this that I want to bring to the surface. Emotions keep you enslaved, and reason makes you free. You can see this more clearly when you reflect that emotions elicit automatic reactions. That's the nature of emotions, to urge you to react without will or intention. That puts you at their mercy if you let it happen.

Reason, on the other hand, is freedom. It's using logic to consider your response and decide how you want to act. That's why we can speak of the "freedom to think" but no one talks about the "freedom of emotion" because that would be a nonsensical statement. If you're not intellectually free, no other aspect of your life will be free.

You now have a solid overview of the trivium, know the commitments and core values that support practicing it, and the proper role of emotions. The next three chapters go into each of the arts in more depth.

Chapter 4

KNOWLEDGE STARTS WITH A COMMITMENT TO ACCURACY

B reaking down words into their constituent parts can be illuminating. For example, the word knowledge is a combination of the words "know" and "ledger." In other words, knowledge is "a ledger of what you know."

Let's take this idea a little deeper. First, ledgers. What are they for? Accountants record figures or data in them. For a ledger to be useful, it needs to be both accurate and as complete as possible. Another thing to note is that we don't ask whether numbers in a ledger are true; instead, we ask whether the numbers are accurate.

This is a remarkably precise analogy for how we should consider the term knowledge as it fits into the trivium. Many people use the word true when they ask about the accuracy of knowledge. That is one sense of the word true, but for our purposes we want to be more precise with our terms.

Truth is a conclusion of logic from accurate premises. We want to think of knowledge as input data which we analyze for accuracy. We should reserve the word truth for useful outputs produced after we correctly process inputs.

One reason to do this is because a fact (or piece of knowledge) can be technically accurate but is highly misleading without additional facts around it. When we speak loosely and say that a specific piece of knowledge is true, it can be distorting.

Instead, you should think of yourself as collecting as much accurate knowledge as possible, to then be systematically configured or processed by logic into something that's true.

In other words, the true meaning of "know-ledge" requires that what is known be accurate and complete.

Let's stick for the moment on this idea of manipulating knowledge. A few examples could help get the point across.

It could be a newscast excoriating a country as "warmongers" for declaring war on another nation. The fact of declaring war is accurate, but the implication may not be. What if England had been portrayed as a "warmonger" for declaring war on Germany in 1939? In one light, it could be presented as true, but only by omitting facts about Germany repeatedly breaking pledges and aggressively invading other countries prior to the declaration of war.

You can also see manipulation like this with ordinary examples from everyday life. Say you're talking to a salesman who gives you accurate facts about his product. But he's leaving out knowledge that there is a competing product that performs identically at half the cost. This is why it's important to see knowledge as facts being recorded in a ledger. Once you have all the relevant entries in the ledger, you can then use logic to put them together to ask what is true. If you try to make a truth claim out of an incomplete ledger, you're going to make bad decisions.

Here's another example from the world of healthcare. You're informed that your gallbladder is malfunctioning. Let's accept that this is an accurate premise (assuming you're seeing a competent medical professional). Next, the surgeon tells you that your condition will require surgery. The surgeon has just made a truth claim using only that one piece of limited knowledge.

The knowledge that "the gallbladder is malfunctioning" is indeed correct or an accurate premise. However, the conclusion that it "requires surgery" may or may not be true. Here's the knowledge being left out:

- A surgeon wants to perform surgeries as a matter of self-interest, both financially and professionally.
- A holistic practitioner could give you an additional accurate fact that a vitamin and mineral deficiency is causing the problem and that you have other options.

Of course, you may enter all the entries necessary into your ledger, apply logic, and in some cases still come to the conclusion that surgery is your best option. But without understanding the distinction between input (knowledge) and output (truth expressed as wisdom), your decision will be rooted in confusion, not logic.

Are there times when you can't get a complete enough picture to make a sound decision? Of course. Sometimes it's just a matter of needing more time for more knowledge to be collected. That's another reason why a commitment to the voice of reason over emotion is so crucial. Important decisions are a process and should be deliberative—accept that good decisions take time.

There will be other times, of course, when you can't get all the knowledge you'd like. That's when some people fall into the dangerous fallacy of futility: "I can't know everything, so why bother knowing anything?"

This is a poor excuse for giving up on intellectual rigor. Don't stop reasoning because you can't know everything.

Understanding Science

The huge role of science in our world can hardly be overstated. Which is why it's especially disheartening that so many people have a fundamental misunderstanding of what science actually is. This misapprehension about how science works is precisely because people don't make this distinction between knowledge and truth.

Sadly many people think of science as finalized judgments that are authoritatively announced from on high by unquestioned experts. Under this conception of science, it would be considered blasphemy to practice healthy skepticism and question the conclusions of current science.

True scientists understand that science is never "final," and that the very heart of science is questioning its provisional conclusions again and again. Science is an evolving body of knowledge that constantly strives to get closer and closer to an accurate picture of nature and reality. As new discoveries are made, it is updated. If observations don't match expectations, the body of knowledge must change.

Scientists fully understand that the entries in the ledger need to be as accurate and complete as possible. Without that, it's "garbage in" and "garbage out."

If you doubt that science changes, recall that asbestos was once accepted as safe and effective. So was thalidomide, DDT, and mercury. Thanks to brave and critical thinkers who were immune to the appeal of authority, society has self-corrected these harmful practices. A startling example of this was when Dr. Ignasz Semmelweis recommended washing hands before surgery. His common-sense suggestion has since prevented countless infections, yet at the time he was put in an asylum and humiliated for the crime of "questioning the science."

Checking Knowledge for Accuracy

To this point, we've been mainly focused on whether you have enough entries in your body of knowledge (the ledger of what you know) to begin reasoning. But what about the entries themselves? We need to check those for accuracy, too.

For any given piece of knowledge, the question to ask is, "Empirically, does this statement reflect reality?"

A quick detour to talk about the word "grammar" could be helpful in getting to the heart of this concept. You'll recall that in the Middle Ages and Renaissance, the trivium was referred to as grammar, logic, and rhetoric. Most people have no problem with the word logic. Rhetoric also makes at least some sense as an art. But why the word grammar?

Isn't grammar about when to use a semicolon, or should I capitalize this word, or should it be lay or lie? Yes, but those are specific instances of applied grammar. In its more general sense, grammar is concerned with how words connect to the reality being described.

To put it another way, grammar is concerned with how we define our terms. We need our terms to be agreed upon by all concerned and be consistent in accurately reflecting reality.

Grammar in this larger sense is analogous to data we input into a computer. If the input is inaccurate, a computer can't say, "Oh, I think I know what you mean." The input has to be entered accurately and in the right order or the output will be useless.

In the same way, grammar (the way we use words) has to be an accurate reflection of reality or our own output will be useless, too.

This is why, in the sense we are using it, knowledge can be either right or wrong, but not true or false. The question is simply, does this piece of knowledge accurately reflect reality?

This naturally leads to the idea of how we get knowledge. There are two basic ways: empirical and rational. Empirical knowledge is what we take in through the five senses. It's what we can see, whether a sound is high or low pitched, what something smells like, whether something tastes salty or sweet, or whether it feels smooth or rough.

Then there is rational knowledge, which comes from thought. A good example would be the Pythagorean Theorem: $a^2 + b^2 = c^2$. (C is the hypotenuse side of the triangle, and a and b are the other two sides of the triangle).

Unlike empirical-based knowledge, rational knowledge will not change. In some cases, the context around them will change, but the knowledge always remains accurate. The Pythagorean Theorem states a precise relationship for all time.

For the purposes of making high-quality decisions in everyday life, we need both empirical and rational knowledge, but let's start with empirical knowledge. For example, if you're trying to make a good healthcare decision you need information about your physical condition, like accurate blood test results.

Another real-world example is financial investments. Accurate information that matches reality leads to better decisions (assuming you properly apply logic to the information). A spectacular example of what can go wrong is the infamous Bernie Madoff scandal where the input was completely made up. It was fantasy, with no connection to reality.

Compare that to Warren Buffett, famous for doing his due diligence before investing in anything. Buffet shows what happens when knowledge is grounded in reality and then deliberated upon without emotion. Madoff's victims were provided knowledge that was wildly inaccurate, and the results were catastrophic. These are extreme examples, but the general principle holds in everyday life.

If we are deciding on something, we need to break down every piece of relevant knowledge and ask:

- Is this statement/premise correct?
- And how do I know it is (or isn't)?

Do this as often as possible and the quality of your mind and your life will improve. Ask those two questions again and again.

The Alternative to Checking Your Premises for Accuracy

As a human being, you're going to continually take in knowledge—that's just how we're wired. If you're not acquiring and verifying knowledge empirically and rationally, then you're acquiring it in other ways.

This is where we can return to the idea of the Big 5 institutions and why they are dangerous.

Academia is ready to tell you they've done all the reasoning for you. "Here's the information; spit it back out to us on the exam."

Legacy Media is happy to constantly bombard you with "knowledge" (statements about reality), but they have no interest in providing you a means to evaluate that knowledge. They get more clicks and views with fear, scare headlines, and telling you everything is a "bombshell!" Acquiring knowledge in this heightened emotional state makes you much more susceptible to manipulation.

Big Corporations keep you in a heightened emotional state to get you to buy more. They prey upon your insecurities and weaknesses. Do you want to be as strong as this person? As beautiful? Don't you not need better clothes and the new identity you can have by buying the right products? Slow down and evaluate the premises. You might be surprised what knowledge you're using to make decisions.

Big Tech and Big Government work hand in hand. Governments now openly employ influencers and grant special permissions to social media companies that allow them to operate as so-called "open platforms " while avoiding the responsibility of publishers. This cooperation between tech and government is designed to push a narrative that serves the government's interest, not the public's.

It Won't Be Perfect, But You Will Get Better the More You Practice This

As with all the arts of the trivium, the more you practice identifying knowledge and checking it for accuracy, the better you'll get at it. It's no different from going to the gym. The more you go, the stronger you get.

You also need to accept that there are limits. Just as there are boundaries to physical strength, there are limits to intellectual knowledge. But that's not an excuse to stop training. Tennis pro Roger Federer doesn't stop training even when no one is better. The world's greatest athletes, musicians, and artists never reach complete perfection.

The best will always keep practicing because they understand the value of what they do. You need to understand the value of intellectual rigor and integrity. As you do, it will create a positive feedback loop. When you desire the benefits of reason, you'll work at it and get better. As you get better, you'll understand the value more, and desire it even more.

According to the novelist F. Scott Fitzgerald, "The test of a first-rate intelligence is the ability to hold two opposing ideas in mind at the same time and still retain the ability to function."

Recommended Actions for This Art

Expose yourself to new ideas and experiences by reading nonfiction books and articles, travel to new destinations with different cultures, inquire about other professions and practices foreign to you. As you absorb and accumulate all this new knowledge, do it without accepting it as true or untrue, simply as knowledge from diverse sources to be useful for later application in forming claims/arguments/ conclusions with logic.

Recommended Reading for This Art

Epistemology: A Beginner's Guide by Robert M. Martin

Chapter 5

LOGIC IS POWER

What's the most expensive part of your personal computer or laptop? In almost every case, it's the processor.

In the world of computing, processing power is king. The whole point of a computer is that we give it inputs, and it processes them and then gives us back outputs we can trust. We use the mouse, keyboard, camera, and microphones to provide input. Output to things like printers, speakers, and monitors is only possible after that input has been processed.

Computer technology is now crucial to our lives, and all that innovation and enhancement is firmly rooted in the power of processing. The computer takes input and *uses systematic rules executed according to strict principles* to then provide us reliable output. The value is all in the fact that the processor delivers repeatable, consistent results we can trust.

Logic serves the same function for our minds, and similarly is the fulcrum of the trivium. Like a computer processor, it's the most valuable component. Logic can be defined as *the systematic use of reasoning according to strict principles.* Like that expensive and valuable computer processor, it gives us reliable, repeatable results that can be verified by anyone else using the same principles.

What are the keys to analyzing a problem or concept through the prism of logic?

A little later in this chapter I'll give you some logic basics and some common pitfalls to avoid. But the truth is there's something more important than just learning the rules if you want to be logical.

The first and most important step for using logic is this: you need to commit to exercising personal responsibility for your mind and how it operates.

Make a promise to yourself that you'll think for yourself and make a consistent effort to keep emotions in their proper role. No one is 100 percent perfect in doing this all the time. However, if you pledge to think for yourself using logical principles, you'll get better at it over time.

Some people find this answer disappointing because they're looking for a secret recipe, or a formula that makes everything easy, or anything that takes the pressure off thinking for themselves.

If you're looking to be relieved of the burden of logically thinking for yourself, there's no shortage of people and institutions willing to handle it for you (as has been demonstrated throughout this book). All you have to do is give up ownership of your own mind. The big institutions want to keep you uncommitted, because then you're easier to manipulate.

I won't deny that it's hard to make and keep this commitment to personal responsibility for your own mind, especially when so much of the culture and your intellectual surroundings pull in the opposite direction. But when you genuinely understand what's at stake, committing yourself becomes a necessity.

And what's at stake is nothing less than who you are going to be as a person.

Is your life going to be one reaction after another to whatever wave of emotion is passing over you? Or are you going to be in charge of the quality of your mind?

Will you be listening to whichever arbitrary voice is loudest in your head at any given moment? Or will you firmly bind yourself to the idea of listening to one voice: the voice of reason and logic.

In other words, are you in charge of the quality of your life, or are you surrendering that to the institutions and the culture at large? Recall that the quality of your mind will determine the quality of your decisions, and those decisions will define the quality of your life. Everything is at stake. When you have that insight, committing to logic and reason becomes much easier.

I hope you've already made this commitment to self-responsibility or are at least seriously reflecting on it. Once you've decided you are all in on this commitment, it has two consequences. The first consequence is that you're agreeing to be honest with yourself.

There's a well-documented phenomenon called confirmation bias. It means we tend to recognize evidence that already fits with our beliefs and preferences and overlook or discount facts that cast doubt or disprove our preferred beliefs. It's hard to completely eliminate this bias, but you should be aware of it and always do your best to keep it from skewing your ability to be logical.

What does confirmation bias look like? Here's an example: Let's say you read in a medical journal one week that cow's milk has many harmful effects on your body and contributes to several serious diseases. Then the next month you read a study in that same medical journal about the health benefits of regular consumption of cow's milk.

(These studies back-to-back in the same journal also violate a formal principle in logic, a point we'll get to in a minute.) Which article will you believe?

For most people, the answer depends on whether they like cow's milk or not. If you like drinking it, you'll tend to believe the latter study. If you don't like it or don't drink it, you'll put your faith in the first study.

Confirmation bias can get downright dangerous when not checked, particularly in the area of politics. The more you commit to being honest with yourself and are willing to take into account your own preconceived ideas and inclinations, the more logical you'll become.

There's a second consequence that follows from your dedication to personal responsibility: a commitment to brutal honesty with yourself about your current ability to be logical. When I'm coaching someone or talking to someone after my lectures, I'll sometimes ask, "Are you a logical thinker?"

Most people rate themselves as a "very logical thinker." My follow-up question is, "What are the five operators of logic?" That is almost always met with a blank stare. That tells me they likely don't understand the ancient art of logic, and they are likely not as logical as they think. They can get there, but you can't fix what you don't know is a problem. That's why you need to be honest about where you are in your understanding of logic.

Don't get me wrong. You do not need an advanced degree in logic to be a reasonable person. Your knowledge of logic just needs to have sufficient depth to understand the basic principles of the subject and a commitment to practicing them.

Learning the Basics of Logic

Stunningly logic is not considered a major subject of study in our education system. (We generally think of a major subject as anything taught in most schools. So math, history, and language arts all qualify, but logic does not.)

This ignorance of logic as a field of study allows most people to walk through the world and their life thinking, "I'm a fairly logical person," when the truth is they've never been taught and never explored the basic operations of logic. This idea that "we already know logic" is a great barrier to learning it, because we don't know that there's some basic training we've missed out on.

First, let's cover inductive and deductive reasoning.

Inductive Reasoning

Inductive reasoning is all about gathering observations and using them to form a theory. You begin with the specific facts you gather (things you've taken in through the senses, what you've seen, heard, and otherwise observed) and then you put them together into a conclusive argument or claim.

Inductive reasoning is most useful going from the specific to the abstract. Here's a simple example to get the point across:

- I **observe** that I enjoy pizza.
- When I'm at a pizza restaurant, I **observe** all the people there enjoying pizza.
- **Conclusion:** Therefore, all people enjoy pizza.

Notice that the conclusion is actually false. The basic form of this inductive argument is correct, but it goes wrong because the conclusion goes beyond the observations. The conclusion should have been: *some* people enjoy pizza.

Here's another example. Let's say you hear about a study involving fifty mice, and the researchers are testing out a treatment for a disease. During the experiment, thirty-five of the mice show improvement. Therefore, the researchers conclude that the treatment is 70 percent effective and further theorize that humans will see similar results.

There are two big issues with their conclusion. First, a small sample size of fifty is not enough to confidently support the conclusion for an entire species. Secondly, it is an even bigger logical stretch to conclude that a completely different species (humans) would yield similar results.

Just from these simple examples, you can see the potential for problems. I also hope that you see that inductive arguments get stronger with more observations (knowledge/facts). The more knowledge you gather, the more likely your inductive conclusion will be true.

Deductive Reasoning

Deductive reasoning works best in the opposite way. You start with a premise that is an abstraction (not an observation) that makes a claim to be self-evidently true.

Then you add an accurate observation. When you add the first premise to the second premise, you form an inescapable conclusion (assuming the accuracy of both premises).

The classic example (seemingly included in almost every logic textbook ever written) will illustrate a deductive argument:

- **Abstract premise that is self-evidently true:** All men are mortal.
- **Observed premise:** Socrates is a man.
- **Conclusion:** Therefore, Socrates is mortal.

These are the two most basic forms of logical arguments. You should also know the five operators of logic:

LOGICAL NEGATION

- If "Statement A" is true, then "Not Statement A" is false.
- If "Statement A" is false, then "Not Statement A" is true.

This is logic at its most basic. Something cannot be both true and false at the same time. Yes, that's incredibly simple, but when you break down arguments, you'd be surprised how many times you see a very fundamental contradiction.

LOGICAL CONJUNCTION (AND)

For a conjunction to be true, both statements being conjoined must be true.

- If "Statement A" is true, *and*
- If "Statement B" is true
- *Then* the conjunction "A and B" is also true.

For example:

- A = An aardvark has four legs.
- B = A bull has horns.

Therefore, the conjunction "An aardvark has four legs and a bull has horns" is true. However, if instead "B = a bull has wings," then the conjunction "A and B" is false.

LOGICAL DISJUNCTION (INCLUSIVE OR)

For a disjunction to be true, only one of the statements must be true. If either statement is true then the disjunction is true.

For example:

- A = An aardvark has four legs.
- B = A bull has wings.

Therefore, the disjunction "An aardvark has four legs or a bull has wings" is true. A disjunction is only false when both statements A and B are false. While obvious when you see it in this form, statements in everyday life can be manipulative by playing with the word "or."

LOGICAL IMPLICATION (CONDITIONAL)

If "Statement A" is true, then "Statement B" is true.

If I vote for candidate A, then taxes will go up. Simple enough. But people will use something that sounds like this logical operation that doesn't actually work.

A politician may say, if you elect A, then all these terrible things will happen. But you need to break down what he's claiming will happen and see if it logically follows.

LOGICAL BICONDITIONAL (DOUBLE IMPLICATION)

This one has many more complicated forms, but the most basic is: "Statement A" is true if and only if "Statement B."

The only way "Statement B" could be true is if "Statement A" is true, and the only way "Statement A" could be true is if "Statement B" is true.

As you grow in your understanding of logic, you'll get better and better at breaking down arguments into these categories and assigning them as propositions and seeing if they logically make sense.

This will help you see through some of the most common strategies used to manipulate people. These tricks can be seen most clearly in the world of politics. For example, you hear it said, "If you support more border enforcement, then you are a racist."

There are several ways you could link these two statements:

- You are for more border enforcement and your motivation is racism.
- You are for more border enforcement, and you are a racist, but your motivation for wanting more border enforcement is independent of your racism.

- You're for more border enforcement and you are not a racist.
- Flipping it around, you could be a racist and be for less border enforcement.

If all these things could be true, baldly stating that supporting more border enforcement automatically leads to a conclusion of racism is logically false. Another way of saying it: if all these things could be true, is there any value or fairness in assuming a connection between more border enforcement and racism? In summary, there may be many reasons to support border enforcement that are not racist; therefore, to conclude that one is racist simply for supporting border enforcement is a fallacy.

Reach for Logical Conclusions

Our politics would be healthier if we could identify premises and connect them to logical conclusions, instead of using emotionally charged words to imply conclusions that don't logically connect.

In addition, you can see that the idea of defining terms (part of the knowledge art) can be crucial to reasoning. In this example, many things hinge on what we mean by stronger border enforcement and how we define racism. Having reasoned discussions about definitions is a good starting point to a healthier politics.

Here's another example from the always hot-button political arguments over abortion: Some pro-life advocates use the term "baby-killers" for pro-choice supporters. And some choice advocates are quick to label anyone antiabortion as "misogynists who want to control what women can do with their bodies." With these kinds of inflammatory statements, we're trapped in the world of emotion and have abandoned reason.

A better way is to start by calmly defining terms. What is life and when does it begin? What are the natural rights of the developing fetus and the mother? Define terms and premises and take time to deliberate on how they logically fit together. It's more productive and healthier because it keeps us focused on reason and truth instead of condemning our perceived enemies.

Figuring out how to pull out premises from what people say can be a little like those word problems we used to get in school. From the very simplistic—Johnny has two apples and Janey gives him three apples; how many apples does Johnny have now?—to more complex ones, the idea is the same. You break out the relevant statements, turn them into variables, solve the problem, and then translate it back into words.

What we're doing here is similar, although admittedly more complex than elementary school word problems. When you define terms and break things down logically, you'll start saying things like, "Wait a minute, I'm reading a conclusion for which there are no premises." Or "Those two statements can't both be true at the same time." In other words, by breaking out the statements, you begin to spot errors.

Instead of being overwhelmed with emotional words, you can focus on the accuracy of the statements, how they fit together, and the validity of the claims. Instead of being swept along on a torrent of words and emotional pleas, you're solving a word problem.

It's important to understand that you don't need a graduate-level course in logic to get better at it and get tremendous value out of it. Work on spotting accuracy and consistency of premises and the logic of conclusions every day and you'll be pleasantly surprised by what you learn.

One thing you'll get good at as you practice this is spotting non sequiturs. In logical notation, it would look something like this:

- If A then B.
- If B then C.
- Therefore D is true.

Where did D come from? It came from nowhere, but oftentimes, in a real-world argument, it feels like there should be a connection. So we buy into it, even though that conclusion does not follow from the premises. In more informal reasoning, things are presented as evidence that are often irrelevant or provide very little support for the conclusion.

Here's an example.

- Premise Statement A: Timmy's Tacos is the best restaurant in Amsterdam.
- Premise Statement B: Timmy's Tacos is rated number one in the local newspaper.
- Conclusion: Therefore, Timmy, the owner of Timmy's Tacos, should run for prime minister.

The more you break down articles, speeches, and other forms of communications into their premises and conclusions, you'll see that pulling conclusions out of thin air happens a lot.

More Enemies of Logic

We've identified ignorance of basic logic as a problem. And, of course, we've identified the manipulative big institutions as another problem.

But there are also some other cultural currents that are generating further resistance to reason. One of the biggest is we've created a society that makes all of us feel perpetually short on time.

Things do move fast, but much of that speed is manufactured through manipulation. "You've got to decide to buy this shiny object right now!" or "*Ding.* Check your social media feed immediately or you might be missing out on something important going on."

This distracted, always-short-on-time mindset is the exact opposite of what we need in order to act logically. We can still make efficient decisions, but we need to slow down enough for good, quality deliberation. If politicians are talking, we need to stop long enough to break down their statements and figure out what (if anything) they're really saying.

The lack of deliberation when considering political statements is a problem on all ends of the spectrum. For example, sometimes a politician is accused of speaking in coded messages or dog whistles to their base. These accusations aren't helpful. What we should be doing is analyzing what they say and hold them accountable for what they actually said. Conversely, politicians who can skillfully speak using enough vague but positive words can get credit for promising way more than they did. A logical person slows down and analyzes the *actual* statements, then pulls out the premises, and finally asks what conclusions logically follow. (Unfortunately, when you do this, you often find that they said nothing of substance at all.)

Another problem related to the breakneck speed of our culture is that it makes us more susceptible to emotional manipulation, which in turn leads to mental fatigue. If there are multiple institutions keeping you in a state of constant emotional arousal, you end up with tired mental muscles, like a person that has had to tread water too long.

Finally, we're also visually overloaded. There's nothing wrong with some visuals, of course, but too many can wear you down and begin subverting your cognitive ability. Emotion is also easier to elicit with visuals and that makes you more reactive and less responsive.

The ultimate goal is to be able to take all the information flying at us and be able to pull out the premises, and then evaluate them based on stable and reliable rules. As we discourse with friends, read articles, listen to political rhetoric, and more, let's turn down the emotional volume and turn up reason.

As political philosopher Thomas Paine wrote, "The most formidable weapon against errors of every kind is reason."

When You Are Too Emotional to
Be Logical, Give Yourself a Break

All through this book, I've been urging you to take full responsibility for the quality of your mind and to be vigilant about not letting emotions take over your life.

But I also don't want to portray this as uniformly easy all the time. One of my weaknesses is putting too much pressure on myself for my reasoning to be flawless in every situation. Flawless reasoning is a good goal to aim for as long as you realize it's not always attainable. Strive for it, but don't let falling short on occasion discourage you.

You also will have times in your life where you've suffered severe emotional trauma. Maybe a parent just died and you're off balance. Maybe the issue up for discussion is violence against women and you're a rape victim. Maybe someone is gaslighting you in a particularly vicious way.

Give yourself a break if you slip up. If the debate is on an issue where you have deep personal scars, maybe you need to do some more healing before jumping in.

Always stay committed to logic, but allow that you're human, too. As I've said before, emotions are not the enemy, we just need to acknowledge them and use them as feedback.

Now that you've learned how to assess knowledge and

apply logic, it's time to figure out the best ways to get more truth out into the world.

Recommended Actions for This Art

Try to suspend the desire to make hasty conclusions. Practice asking more questions to acquire more knowledge and deeper understanding prior to drawing conclusions. Make a habit of thoroughly evaluating premises prior to accepting or drawing conclusions. Play games that require methodological thinking and problem-solving.

Recommended Reading for This Art

Introducing Logic: A Graphic Guide by Dan Cryan, Sharron Shatil, and Bill Mayblin

Chapter 6

RHETORIC IS NOT (ALWAYS) A DIRTY WORD

R hetoric has become a (mostly) bad word in our culture. The word is now almost exclusively associated with manipulation, the classic example being long-winded political types telling us dressed-up lies.

It wasn't always this way. In ancient cultures and in the Middle Ages and Renaissance, rhetoric was usually considered a valuable skill that a person was admired for mastering (although Socrates had some serious objections to rhetoricians, a point he made with great rhetorical skill!).

Why the two different takes on the word rhetoric, one admiring and one negative? This isn't just a case of a word evolving in meaning. The two different perspectives on the word point to a real conflict in the concept of rhetoric itself.

Rhetoric has a double-edged nature, and which way it cuts hinges on who's wielding the sword. Rhetoric can be moral or immoral, depending on the intention of the person deploying it.

When someone uses skillful communication techniques to impart a truth rooted in the hard work of knowledge gathering and logical processing, then it's a force for good.

When someone utilizes rhetorical techniques in order to manipulate without regard to the truth or falseness of what he's saying, we see the ugly side of rhetoric.

Using Rhetoric in the Right Way

Let's begin with the ethical use of rhetoric. Within the structure of the trivium, rhetoric is the way to share the output (or wisdom). If you've done the hard work of gathering knowledge and checking it for accuracy, and if you've processed it using strict rules of logic and understanding, now it's time to share the wisdom you've earned. This is your output, and the world needs to receive it in a persuasive form, because the world needs more reason and truth.

This is the positive side of rhetoric, the act of an ethical person who has reasoned his way to truth and wants to use proven techniques to transmit truth and influence people.

I'm not going to teach you the technical terms of rhetoric (there are a lot of them). Instead, I'm going to give you a few simple ways to positively influence people. You'll notice that most of my advice in this area tilts towards communicating with people one-on-one.

This is for two reasons. For one, I think this is the most effective setting for persuasion. Second, it's better to sharpen your skills under less pressure first. As you grow more into the trivium, you'll get more comfortable talking to larger groups and persuading in speeches or presentations.

Persuasion Techniques That Work

One of my favorite techniques called "staying in agreement" was taught to me by a mentor. This is where you avoid putting people in a defensive posture using phrases like "you're wrong" or doing a frontal assault on their position.

Instead, you walk someone through each step of a logical argument, checking for agreement each step of the way. When you directly attack someone and make it personal ("*You are wrong*"), you're charging that person up with emotion and putting them in a reactive state instead of a receptive one.

There's another form of staying in agreement that's also effective, and that's by parrying their attack of you by acknowledging at least part of their point. It defuses emotion. For example, if a wife says to her husband, "Bill, you're a jerk," Bill could respond, "Yeah, you know, you're right; I sometimes am a jerk."

What's going to happen? In most cases, this agreement begins to calm the situation. The fight part is over, and now the couple has a chance to talk about the underlying issues in a more reasoned way.

Another persuasion technique is mirroring. If you're in a discussion with another person, try mirroring their breathing patterns, sitting positions, use of hands, and tilt of head. It's proven to build rapport, which is the right tone for a reasoned discussion. (I hope it's obvious that you want to be subtle about mirroring and not end up looking like you're mocking the other person!)

Another way to persuade is to listen. The natural human tendency when trying to persuade is to want to talk more. After all, how can you persuade someone if you sit there silently?

The truth is that genuinely listening is rare (and becoming rarer). If you do practice listening, you'll stand out because most people aren't used to really being heard. As the other person talks, don't be constantly thinking of your rebuttal or your own point; instead, listen with the intention of understanding the other person as thoroughly as possible. Either you will learn that you are not actually in disagreement at all, or that there is possibly more knowledge relevant to the discussion that is yet to be acquired. And if you strongly disagree with something someone says, don't react with disgust or sarcasm. The other person will react in kind or shut down completely.

A better approach rather than disdain is to repeat things back for understanding, even things you don't agree with. This works for two reasons: one, the person sees that you're paying attention to what they're saying and showing sincere interest, which makes them feel good. It also starts to lower their ego-driven defense mechanisms and makes them more open to staying engaged in the discussion and more open to your ideas, which by now are more likely to be based on logic and reason. Also, when you rephrase something, you're giving the person back a gift. You may be widening their perspective on it or giving them more ways to explain their own thoughts.

All of the above are persuasion techniques, but they're more than that, too. When you keep things calm, stay in agreement, mirror the other person, and show respect by listening, you're reminding yourself to keep your own emotions under control and truly honor the other person's point of view. In short, using these techniques is a discipline for keeping yourself reasonable, too. Simply extend the same courtesy that you would expect and enjoy from others in a sincere and mutual attempt to increase individual knowledge and understanding.

What about setting? We can't always choose the circumstances of a discussion, but when we can choose, there are settings that are more conducive to persuasion and the reasonable exchange of ideas. The absolute ideal setting is one-on-one with a trusted colleague, friend, or partner, and with no distractions.

On the other end of the spectrum, the absolute worst situation for healthy communication is being talked at, while distractions are flying at you, too. For example, overproduced television shows with a newscaster lecturing, all while other messages scroll across the screen. The newscasters are always dressed to a T, not a hair out of place, and the screen subtly flickers (even though you can't perceive it). The total effect is much closer to conditions of hypnosis than genuine communication.

Communication and persuasion require two parties. That's not happening via the screen when the content coming out of it is not food for thought, but instead is prepackaged thoughts and ideas. In a culture dedicated to constantly putting consumable content in front of you, how can you get better at reasoned discussion and sharing your wisdom?

The answer used to be Academia, but those days are gone. Now Academia is trapped in a tunnel vision of ideology instead of a commitment to truth. You can find a good professor here and there, but even they have pressure to conform; it's often a threat to their financial well-being for the pseudo crime of expressing any ideology unapproved by the academic authorities.

My suggestion is to turn to older literature. Read the Greeks and the Stoics. Aristotle is good on both logic and rhetoric. Make the effort to read actively; when you do, you enter into a conversation.

Another way to sharpen your output skills is to form groups with people who also practice reasoned debate and the liberal arts. This has the added benefit of keeping you energized and motivated. I run a Facebook group that does this, and I also look to cultivate friendships with people who respect reason. One of the finest qualities to find in someone is their prioritization of acquiring knowledge and understanding above reputation or winning a debate.

Look for ways to do similar things. This goes back to the idea of self-reliance and self-responsibility that I've mentioned several times in relation to the trivium. When you can't find what you need in Academia or Mainstream Media, go out and help create your own communities.

Seeking out others who practice reason and understand objective truth will sharpen your skills and boost your enjoyment. In a way, when you have two people who have learned the skills of the trivium, it's like doubling your processing power. Your database of accurate knowledge is bigger, as well.

We must take this art seriously, because if we're poor at it, people who need the trivium and its benefits are going to be turned off. We're going to be keeping something valuable from them.

Stop Worrying about Winning

Of course, there will be situations where you do your best to set up a reasoned dialogue and it just doesn't work. When this happens, I recall a famous Thomas Paine quote: "To argue with a man who has renounced the use and authority of reason, and whose philosophy consists in holding humanity in contempt, is like administering medicine to the dead, or endeavoring to convert an atheist by scripture."

However, I do encourage you to not give up on healthy dialogue with people, even if they are not receptive to reason right off. Work at it to your threshold, and that threshold may increase as you get better at putting reason in charge of your actions.

Another thing I tell people whom I coach is this: stop worrying about convincing the other person. Instead look at it as an opportunity to practice your rhetorical skills and develop your abilities. Look at it as a challenge to persuade, but let go of the need to "win."

That's the biggest reason you get frustrated: you want to win. We all do. But give up any expectation that you're going to change their mind. Focus on the skills, and do the best job you can, using reason as your touchstone. If that still fails, you did everything you could. Let it go. If you are still concerned with winning, then focus on the victory of being better than you were previously. After all, you are your greatest competition.

Protecting Yourself against Rhetoric

At the top of this chapter, I said rhetoric has two faces. If a person is a skilled rhetorician, they can make the worse argument appear the stronger, particularly if the listeners are weak in the liberal arts.

One of the most common examples of manipulative rhetoric is the use of talismanic words. Politicians in particular use this all the time, but the use of talismanic words is more widespread than just politics. Talismanic words are vague terms like hope, forward progress, change—words that can mean almost anything unless specifics are provided.

This rhetorical trick works because these words have positive and uplifting connotations, while being essentially void of meaning. And the speakers know that the void will be filled with meaning by the listeners, who want to feel good about what they are hearing.

As poet and diplomat Octavio Paz said, "The relations between rhetoric and ethics are disturbing: the ease with which language can be twisted is worrisome, and the fact that our minds accept these perverse games so docilely is no less cause for concern."

Some common techniques to watch out for:

Straw Man Argument

This occurs when someone restates an argument or claim in a distorted way and then attacks the weakness of the distortion.

Example: Senator Adams says that the nation should not open the borders. Senator Barnes says that he is disappointed that Senator Adams hates and fears foreigners.

It may be that Senator Adams loves and embraces foreigners, but merely wants to better account for their admission to the country in order to ensure their safety and proper rights or benefits. Senator Barnes, however, distorts Senator Adams's claim to make him appear hateful and unappealing.

Appeal to Authority

The validity of reasoned arguments cannot be contingent on the person or institution making that argument. Reason is rooted in logically combining premises and has nothing to do with the person stating those premises. Watch out for subtle versions of this.

Example 1: Leading scientists and many scientific research papers show that smoking cigarettes is not addictive and does not cause cancer. (It is not scientists or even research papers that prove something true. It is accurate premises combined logically.)

Example 2: Professor Dinkley is the foremost leading biologist in the world and he says that evolution is true. (Evolution may or may not be true. However, if it is true, it is not because an expert stated that it is true, but because of the preponderance of evidence.)

Social Conformity

Often couched as a "call to the greater good," this is actually a means of enforcing social behaviors the speaker wants to control.

Example: A lot of people think this politician is homophobic, therefore this politician is homophobic. (What people "think about" a politician does not define the truth of statements about the politician.)

Appeal to Emotions

Is a speaker calling on your pity, your revulsion, or your "wanting it to be true" to persuade you? If what they are proposing doesn't logically solve what they claim, don't get swayed by emotional appeals.

Example: The claim is that electrical power lines cause cancer. If someone says, "My seven-year-old son died of cancer and we live fifteen kilometers from electrical power lines. Just before he died in agonizing pain he asked me if I would fight to have those electrical power lines removed so that no more children would have to suffer like him." (While you could obviously sympathize with this speaker, nothing in the statement proves the claim.)

Linguistic Fallacies

Watch out for anyone intentionally using the multiple meanings of words (or the slippery definitions of some words) to try to persuade you.

Red Herrings

Red herrings are false paths, essentially the fallacy of relevance.

Example: A leader's personal character traits are often irrelevant to their morality as leaders. Hitler famously loved dogs, a trait we usually associate with kindness and a good heart. I think you can see how ridiculous this is. (Watch

what a leader does and what policies they are implementing; stop worrying about whether you like them.)

Legacy Media loves to portray people in caricatures of
either good or evil, and then link those character issues
with substantial policy issues.

Another similar example: celebrities have more influence
than they've earned because they play characters we identify with on stage, screen, and TV. We see them in roles as
the protective father, the nurturing mother, or the loveable
maverick. We feel a rapport with them, which makes us
more susceptible to adopting their opinions or giving their
pronouncements undue weight.

Politicians who can come across as particularly sincere on
screens have a similar advantage. Your job as an individual
of reason is to be aware of these subtle cues and filter them
out. Do not allow yourself to be distracted by irrelevancies.

We've now covered the basics of the trivium. The next
four chapters are devoted to how these ideas can play out
in the real world in four key areas of life: business, relationships, healthcare, and politics.

Recommended Actions for This Art

Familiarize yourself with some of the most popular informal fallacies. This way you can avoid using them yourself,

and also spot them when used by others. Besides the ones mentioned in this chapter, look out for other fallacies, including: Ad Populum (Bandwagon Argument), Circular Reasoning, the Genetic Fallacy, Anecdotal Evidence, the Slippery Slope, Non Sequitur, Tu Quoque, Projection, the Middle Ground, and the Gambler's Fallacy.

Recommended Reading for This Art

How to Win an Argument: An Ancient Guide to the Art of Persuasion by Marcus Tullius Cicero and James M. May.

Chapter 7

BUSINESS
AND WORK

L et's say you're a young or inexperienced but highly motivated entrepreneur with a deep desire for success. You're making your fair share of mistakes, and money is getting tight.

In addition to the dread of embarrassing failure looming over you, maybe you have a family depending on you. Personal bills are stacking up right next to business costs. Whether or not you're showing it on the outside, you've got a lot of anxiety about whether you'll ever crack the code and build a business that's a long-term success. As the pressure mounts, it can be hard to control the emotion of fear.

So you start hunting for answers. You see an online course promising to teach you the secrets of successful entrepreneurship. You read through the sales page and become increasingly excited. "This is it," you think to yourself. "This is exactly what I need."

Well, maybe.

We'll get back to the problems with this scenario in a moment, but first let me tell you a little about my own journey as an entrepreneur.

Today, I run several successful healthcare practices in the Netherlands, but I struggled quite a bit at the beginning.

When I finished my postgraduate degree, I was convinced that my newly acquired skills plus the degree would give me everything I needed to successfully open my own clinic. I was naïve enough to believe that if I offered a good service at a fair price, people would just show up.

I knew and understood healthcare, but I failed to comprehend that the *business* of healthcare is a completely different thing. It came as a shock to me that my business struggled like crazy. My savings evaporated, and things were getting tight.

Then I got lucky. Or at least I thought I did. A well-meaning person offered me free advice. It helped me lower my prices, and clients flocked to my practice. Things took off and I was thrilled.

That euphoria turned out to be short-lived. At the end of the year, I found out I was losing money. I wasn't charging enough to make a profit. Not only did I feel foolish, but genuine fear and panic started to grip me.

I kicked myself for just blindly taking free advice. The saying "cheap advice is no good, and good advice is not cheap" is true. But I never blame a coach or advisor, free or paid. It's up to me to do my due diligence. And I hadn't done that.

The ego has some healthy aspects, and one of those is that your self-image rebels against total failure. Some failure along the way is expected in business, but I didn't want the entire ship to go down. So I had to go out in search of better advice. After some better research, I hired a terrific coach, and my business improved dramatically.

Interestingly, one of the first things this coach did was help me define terms. (Notice the connection to the trivium, where the art of knowledge requires defining terms accurately.) Previously, I always assumed I knew what marketing was, but I'd never precisely defined it. Once I got clear on the definition, I applied logic to understand it, and then I implemented it (my output).

This inspired me to apply the trivium to as many aspects of my business as I could. It worked wonders, and I've never stopped using it. For decisions both large and small, my goal is to always use reason and not let emotions interfere in the decision-making process.

I want to pause for a moment and point out the valuable role emotion did play in all this. As I said, fear and panic grabbed me when the year-end books showed I was losing money. That's a sign of emotion doing its job. It was good feedback. You should feel something deeply when your business is failing, and it should be unpleasant.

What changed was what I did with that emotional feedback. The first time I was worried about my business, I blindly reacted by taking the first free advice that came along and sounded good. But the second time, I thanked the emotions for the feedback. Then I pushed them aside, slowed down long enough to find an excellent coach, and started responding to the situation with reason.

My emotions were correct. I was in an upsetting position, but if I had continued to make decisions in the grip of fear, that would've only made things worse.

Let's circle back to the young entrepreneur who was ready to buy the online course to improve his business and rid himself of the anxiety of failure. Let's stipulate that his emotions are a valid gauge of an actual problem: he needs to learn the right skills to avoid his business failing.

The problem comes in when the young entrepreneur makes the emotional decision to buy the online course fast, without gathering enough knowledge about it and then thinking it through logically. All logic gets short-circuited by the feeling of relief he gets from buying the course that he believes is going to solve his problems.

Many times, what's happening is you're trying to outsource a hard decision. I've made that mistake myself in moments of pressure and anxiety. We think we're making a reasonable decision to improve our business, but we're not doing our due diligence about what we're buying. We hope the course will show us exactly what to do, with no need to do the thinking for ourselves or make our own tough decisions.

Of course, many coaches and courses are worthwhile. As I indicated, I've used these resources myself and they've helped me. I also do coaching myself, so I definitely believe in the value. But you need to gather the knowledge first, and logically think it through.

Here's some advice for analyzing offers to help your business. This isn't meant to be a complete list, but rather a window into how to use reason to make better decisions:

- Beware of advice that is rooted mainly in inspirational platitudes like "follow your gut" or "you have to have courage to be an entrepreneur." While at times well-meaning and having a kernel of truth, this advice often crosses over into magical thinking, as if the power of your belief will be enough to make your business successful. Courage is wonderful, but in business, calculated courage is better. Courage in absence of reason will equal destruction.

• Acquire knowledge about the method of teaching or coaching. Is it audio? Mostly reading? One-on-one in-person coaching? Then consider whether the format matches how you learn best.

• Gather knowledge about the teacher or coach. Investigate their qualifications. Look deeper into testimonials—not only what they say, but who is saying it.

• How are they using the word entrepreneur? The word is becoming more and more devalued by people who are selling quick-money schemes, more interested in perceived success than in putting in hard work for actual success.

After you've gathered knowledge, begin evaluating with logic:

- Is what's being offered something where you already know what to do and you're just not doing it? Are you tempted to purchase it thinking it will be a way to buy your way out of doing the work?

- Is what it teaches a weakness of yours? In other words, will this help you where you need it?

- Think of all the different things a course could be. It could be a scam. It could be a bad course. It could be a quality course that doesn't fit your needs. It could be a quality course, but the value doesn't match the price. Or it could be a quality course that suits your needs and is priced fairly. The last is the only one you should say yes to. Even a good course should be turned down if it doesn't match your needs.

It's my hope that you see how slowing down and applying reason is a far better mindset to make a decision than getting excited and making a purchase in a heightened emotional state.

Of course, analyzing available coaches and courses is just one use of the trivium for entrepreneurs. Every decision in your business should go through this process. Good business coaches are using this process all the time without being aware of its name. At heart, coaches teach you to acquire facts, analyze the consequences, and then implement the new policy/procedure/action.

Here's an example: let's say you want to improve your customer's journey, so you can capture more sales, and get increased repeat and referral business.

First step, gather knowledge:

- What do we currently know about our customer's journey?
- What steps do we need to take to gather more knowledge about that journey?
- What are the relevant facts we need to complete an avatar or profile of our ideal customer?
- Where are we losing potential customers along the journey?

Next, start logically thinking through this process and use reasoning to think about ways to improve it. For example, instead of just asking where on the journey you are losing potential customers or clients, you ask *why* you're losing them. You'll come up with ideas to improve.

Don't immediately implement those ideas. Look at what you're proposing to implement and logically evaluate the likely consequences. When you've exhausted all you can do in terms of collecting knowledge and applying logic, it's time to make a decision and take action.

Confident Decisions

How does the third part of the trivium fit with entrepreneurship? Your output, or wisdom, is your business *decisions*. As an entrepreneur, you need to be hyper decisive. The more you lay the groundwork with knowledge and logic, the more confidence you'll have in your decisions.

This is especially valuable because successful entrepreneurship often means having the patience to stick to a decision. Just like it takes time for a child to mature into an adult, a business needs time to grow and mature. If you've made your decisions in good faith and using reason, you won't fall into the trap of changing things every time you have an emotional whim.

Of course, it's always a balance. If you find yourself losing money at year's end, you know you must make changes. But as you grow in your ability to reason, you'll begin to trust your decisions more, and won't panic or overreact to setbacks.

Setbacks

Setbacks are going to happen, even when using the trivium. When they do, apply the trivium to what went wrong.

Gather knowledge about why a certain change increased expenses more than your profit. Figure out what you missed when you made the decision.

Maybe you failed to gather all the relevant facts. Maybe you missed a logical step. It's important to go back and calmly and reasonably figure out where your mistake in thinking was. You'll learn from it.

Once again, notice that emotions are doing their job when you have a setback. They're alerting you to the pain of your mistake. Be glad the emotions are playing their role, then get to work analyzing what went wrong with reason.

Also, know that emotions work both ways. They are also positive feedback. You most likely were motivated by emotion to start a business; that's what passion is. And when you are succeeding, the happiness you feel is excellent feedback.

Other Business Uses

So far, this chapter has been devoted to examples from the world of entrepreneurs. That was intentional, because many of the people who come to me for coaching in the trivium are entrepreneurs. There's a lot of overlap, because people who want to be free and independent in business also want to be free and independent intellectually.

Of course, the trivium is valuable in other areas of business life. Most people have investments, be it a 401(k) or a larger portfolio. Earlier in the book I cited Warren Buffett, who combines meticulous knowledge gathering with logical criteria before investing in any company.

That's how you should be approaching any decision involving personal finance, be it investments or otherwise. Unfortunately, this area is deeply burdened with emotion for many people. There's a reason that money issues are always listed as a top cause of broken marriages. Money is a very emotional issue for many people, but if people brought more reason to it, a lot of problems could be avoided.

The trivium also has value for the day-to-day worker. There are emotional triggers for everyone, no matter what role you have in a business.

I've observed many people who immediately overreact when something goes wrong in their workday. One dissatisfied customer or client sends them into a tailspin. They immediately want to change everything because one mistake was made, or there was one customer who was an exception.

Stop. Breathe. Question the emotions you're feeling and begin to gather knowledge about the situation. Logically look at the consequences of any change you make in your behavior. You'll start to feel more in control at work if you do this.

Another example is in sales. If you have a sales call failure, ask yourself, "Does this sales process usually work?" If the answer is yes, be very careful about any changes you make based on one piece of data (this particular failure).

Look at the sales strategy you used. Maybe it needs to be tweaked. Or maybe you had the right one, but were a little off your game and just executed poorly that day. No need to reinvent the wheel. Slow down, take emotion out of it, and analyze.

Business Knowledge Recommendation

Prior to making any decisions or drawing conclusions, be certain to ascertain as much data and information about the potential business opportunity, investment, employment opportunity, potential hire, or other action. This is commonly referred to as due diligence in business parlance.

As author and web marketing consultant Kevin Stirtz says, "Know what your customers want most and what your company does best. Focus on where those two meet."

Recommended Reading

Traction: Get a Grip on Your Business by Gino Wickman

Business Understanding Recommendation

Once you've gathered as much relevant information as possible (within the bounds of good sense), scan that knowledge for contradictions. Repeat this scan until all contradictions have been resolved without compromising the principles of reasoning. Lastly, be certain that you don't modify your objectives to suit logical inconsistencies; rather, correct the inconsistencies to suit your objective. Have a qualified and trusted independent party check your premises and conclusions.

As the acclaimed actor Laurence Olivier said, "Have a very good reason for everything you do."

Recommended Reading
Principles by Ray Dalio

Business Wisdom Recommendation

Act with decisiveness. Successful people are very decisive and hyperresponsive. Decisiveness is of great value, especially when proper effort is sufficiently invested in both knowledge and understanding beforehand. Once the important work of knowledge and logic has been completed, have the courage to implement—stop hesitating. If consequences are negative or undesired, then accept full responsibility. Do not complain or cast blame. Simply go back and reflect, learn, and repeat the reasoning process.

As uber investor Warren Buffett says, "You only have to do a very few things right in your life so long as you don't do too many things wrong."

Recommended Reading

Predictable Success: Getting Your Organization on the Growth Track—and Keeping It There by Les McKeown

Chapter 8

RELATIONSHIPS

very Sunday night without fail, the wife cooked a ham for dinner. She always prepared it the same way. She cut the ends off the ham, put it in a large pan, and placed it in the oven until it was done.

And every Sunday night at the table, her husband would ask, "Why do you cut off the ends of the ham before cooking it? There's perfectly good meat being cut off."

And she would simply reply, "That's the proper way to cook a ham."

In the interest of a peaceful meal, he would drop the subject. But each Sunday, he repeated the question. It just didn't make any sense to him.

Finally, one Sunday she got tired of him asking and she phoned her mother the next morning. "Mom, when I was growing up, I must've watched a thousand times as you cut off the ends of a ham before you cooked it. Why did you do that?"

"Oh, yes, the ham was always too big for my small pan. So I cut the ends off to make it fit."

There are multiple relationship lessons in this parable. First, there's the relationship between parent and child. The wife in the story had grown up with her mother as an authority figure. That's the proper relationship as a young child, but as adults we need to stop obeying authority and use our own reasoning abilities.

I'm not saying "automatically do the opposite of however you were raised" or anything simplistic like that. There may be some cases where you *should* do the opposite, but the real point is to analyze why you do things. Are you doing something only because it's comfortable and familiar, instead of because it's reasonable?

The blinders need to come off, even in relationships grounded in things like love, parental authority, and trust. Trust is good, but blind faith in any one person, no matter how good that person may be, is not healthy. We need to question our behaviors and how we came to adopt them.

In this story, the cost was a little wasted ham. But we all know there are many situations where the price exacted is much higher. The first step is to take a step back and ask if the knowledge we acquired via our parents is an accurate representation of reality.

There's also a lesson here for intimate relationships. Even in the closest of bonds, we should not be afraid to ask reasonable questions of each other. The husband kept the issue in perspective (it was only ham, after all), but he continued to ask a rational question of his wife. We shouldn't be afraid to raise questions of even our intimate partners. Some people confuse romantic love with a blind faith in the other, as if true love means thinking the other person can do no wrong. This is especially a problem in the early, infatuated stages of a relationship.

You might be thinking, "Shouldn't personal relationships be the one place where emotions *should* be given the upper hand?" No. Emotions certainly matter, but healthy relationships are grounded in reason.

Let's get to the heart of what we want from relationships. With close friends and family, the goal is to enjoy your time with them and to maximize the enjoyment of the time you spend with them. Assuming common values and interests, that enjoyment will happen naturally, except when conflict arises and blocks it.

Unfortunately, we all know that conflict inevitably happens, even in good relationships. So, the overall objective in relationships should be to reduce conflict, which will then allow enjoyment to grow and happen naturally.

But how do you reduce conflict? In my experience, amplifying emotions will only increase the conflict. Turning to reason, on the other hand, improves relationships. The best place to start is with the first art of the trivium: gathering knowledge and defining terms.

Let's say you've started an intimate relationship and your emotions are telling you this is a wonderful person and that this could become a serious relationship. Maybe even a lifetime bond. That's great feedback from your emotions, and you should pay attention. But we also know that emotions are fickle, and a serious commitment needs more grounding than good feelings.

So your emotions are telling you this is a person worth exploring a more committed relationship with. But now you turn to the trivium and begin defining terms. This should be a discussion between you and your potential committed partner.

For example, you should discuss the word "love." It's a beautiful-sounding word that holds a lot of power. But when people hear it, they tend to fill in their own preferred ideal of the word.

When two people in a growing relationship begin to say "I love you" to each other, they may mean two different things. That's why a relationship that feels so good at the beginning can later melt under the pressure of life, to the shock of both parties. They are surprised because they didn't know they had mismatched ideas about the fundamental nature of their relationship.

This is why definitions are so important. Relationship experts talk a lot about the importance of communication, and I agree. Unfortunately, many people think of communicating as "I'll emote to you, and you emote to me." We should talk about emotions, but to solve relationship problems requires commonly defined terms that we can use to reason together. That's how you gain genuine insight.

Another crucial aspect of any serious relationship is to define the roles and expectations you have of each other. How many marriages become embittered because the couple never sat down and had honest conversations to define expectations and responsibilities?

This includes the nitty-gritty details of all the things that need to be done to run a household. The tempting solution is to always split the work and chores fifty-fifty. That sounds good, but in the real world, we know it almost never works out that way.

One spouse gravitates to this duty, one to that chore, and each gets stuck haphazardly with tasks they begrudge. Almost inevitably, resentful emotions build up and the relationship suffers. The root of the problem is that the couple never clearly defined roles and responsibilities. There was also no logic or understanding applied to dividing up the tasks that a household requires. Sometimes that leads to the "output" (the actual task) not getting done at all or being done with bitterness. And that puts emotions in the driver's seat.

I suggest actually writing it out with your partner. That might sound extreme at first, but you'll have a firmer foundation for a lasting relationship if you do. At a minimum, you should have clear, reasoned discussions. The time to do this is before becoming engaged, married, or in a permanent arrangement.

You could discover that your ideas of roles and responsibilities are too far apart to get married. A painful conclusion, no doubt. But much less excruciating than finding out after you've made a lifetime commitment.

Friendship

When it comes to friendships, your goal should be to figure out which ones are worth investing your time in. That might sound a little mercenary or cold, but it's not. To pursue a friendship between incompatible people will inevitably fail.

Sometimes these incompatible "friendships" appear to work on the surface, but that means one or both parties have to violate their own integrity for the sake of the other. That's not friendship, it's a fake copy. What good does that do either person?

Let me give you an example from my own life. I had someone I considered a good friend, and we both loved rock climbing. We would usually participate together in this shared interest at least once a week, sometimes more.

This friendship had formed in the usual way, around a common interest. (After all, we usually don't walk up to someone we barely know and say, "I'm looking for a good friend. Tell me about your core values." No, we say, "You like rock climbing? Me, too. We should get together and climb.")

However, as you spend more time together, core values are going to surface naturally. As you know, one of my bedrock values is a commitment to objective truth. One time while we were climbing, this subject came up.

She startled me by denying objective truth could exist. She was very skeptical that anyone could say what truth was. In her view, it couldn't be defined and did not exist.

As we got deeper into the discussion, I tried my best to show her the meaning of truth and why it mattered. But it quickly became clear that she was an adherent of New Age spirituality and one of her core values was there was no such thing as truth.

I bear this person no ill will, but she and I had a parting of the ways, because I couldn't see investing in a friendship with someone with such a crucial core value diametrically opposed to mine. She told me she believed that deceptions and lies exist, but not their opposite: truth. According to my perspective, that is no different from saying that a door can be open, but it can never be closed. One requires the other.

Believing that lies and falsehoods can exist, but not truth, is a scary worldview in my opinion. My time is valuable to me, and you should value yours as well. It's not enough to share common interests; true friendship requires that core values align. The time you spend forming a surface relationship could be better invested in finding a genuine friend.

When you get to the stage of talking about core values, whether it be with a friend or an intimate partner, I recommend going deeper than words like integrity, responsibility, and honesty. Very few people would claim that they do not value those. Go deeper with questions like, "What do you mean by integrity?" (or whatever value you're talking about).

Finding out about values doesn't have to be something you bring up immediately or directly. It often happens on a more subtle level as you form friendships. Maybe you're out for a few drinks, or attending a sporting event, or shopping, or attending the theater. You're doing things you both enjoy but, in the background, you're tuning into the core values of each other.

What I'm advocating is to bring this search for core values up to the conscious level and truly think about your friendships. Is this a person who shares your values and will be a reliable friend for you? It doesn't necessarily have to be a direct conversation like you'd have with an intimate partner, but the more you can root your connection in shared values and reason, the deeper friendships you'll form.

Notice this is another area where emotions are your guide, but a guide that should be disciplined by reason. Your emotions might be saying, "I'm having a good time with this person. Underneath, I feel some anxiety about the values (or behavior) this person is exhibiting, but I want to get along and not stop feeling good." Logic should take that feedback and ask, "What is behind this uneasiness? Can I define it?"

When you analyze a friendship, you can take action based on your understanding, by either continuing to deepen the friendship or extricating yourself from it. Emotions can help you measure but should not be decisive.

Family

Your relationship with your family is usually the most emotional bond of all. While some families are relatively harmonious, others experience significant conflict. Yet, even in challenging situations, families often find ways to come back together.

That's because while there are often surface tensions based on dissimilar interests, we return to each other because underneath the conflicts, core values are shared. Shared values make sense, because the first place you begin learning values is within the family. Then as you reached adulthood, you left to pursue your own future and interests, and to think through your own values.

This initial launching into the world at large is often accompanied by a break in relations. It could be a subtle gap, or it could be very open and painful. Sometimes these breaks can be extended, but in the end, common values usually bring us together.

Here's what I recommend in situations of conflict with family: First, keep your integrity. This calls back to the idea of maintaining internal order and letting external chaos be. You may have a sibling who is wayward, or parents who want to preserve authority over you. Or any number of other issues where you'll be tempted to let emotions rule.

Separate yourself as much as needed to maintain your own internal freedom, order, and integrity. That must always be the priority. But I also recommend not shutting the door on family (except in the most extreme cases). Draw your own internal lines and don't forget that shared values are eventually remembered, but use those limits to keep from getting manipulated emotionally.

This is also a good place to add that if you begin regularly practicing the trivium, you're going to get better at it, and that means you'll likely exceed your family, friends, and significant others in your ability to reason and find truth. But it's important to guard against a refusal to reevaluate your own positions. The trivium is a perfect system, but our use of it is not.

Having the humility to reevaluate your own reasoning and conclusions is not the same as falling into the trap of relativism, the false notion of "my truth" and "your truth." Stick to your conclusions when warranted, but listen to the definitions of others and see if you need to reconsider.

Also, keep hatred out of relationships. I've had some experience in my own family where for a period of time we weren't in close contact. I had truth commitments that I had considered deeply and wasn't willing to sacrifice them to make others comfortable.

But, and this is key, I didn't feel or express hatred or anger toward my family. The door was left open. Eventually, they began to see things happening in the world that made them reconsider their own ideas and they came much closer to my conclusions. Shared values kicked back in. And because bridges hadn't been burned, there was reconciliation. Leave open the possibility of family relationships blossoming again.

Getting Even More Practical

Let me end this chapter by giving you some more ideas for staying reasonable in relationships.

Relationships are the place where emotions tend to boil over faster and harder than other areas. In other words, you're going to mess this up. I still do. We all have a threshold of tolerance, and then emotions override judgment and take the form of yelling, aggressive body language, and other unhelpful actions.

When that happens, it's not worth trying to use the trivium again until you calm down. Give yourself time because you won't be able to evaluate the relationship in an emotional state. But once you've become truly calm, go back and apply the trivium.

Gather knowledge: How did the conflict start? Was it a matter of not defining terms? Were the terms agreed upon, but a wrong step was taken in logic?

I explicitly use the trivium when discussing my relationships with others. But that's not absolutely necessary. You can do these steps without introducing the terms of the trivium.

In fact, good relationship counselors use the methods that align with the trivium. A successful relationship counselor will begin by steering a couple toward a shared understanding of terms.

Interestingly, many counselors also encourage healthy rhetoric. For example, they advise to not speak in statements that tell the other person how they feel and to not engage in direct personal attacks. It's another instance where the trivium is revealed as the natural way that a healthy mind operates.

Another valuable asset for bringing more reason to relationships is sincere apologies. Apologies are like a dial that turns emotions down, opening a space for reason to reassert itself.

Of course, insincere apologies to keep the peace are a bad idea. The conflicts will keep happening because you're sacrificing truth and integrity. Remember that an individual who avoids conflict simply to keep the peace will eventually start a war within themselves.

There will be times when you don't think you were wrong in the argument, but you realize you reacted poorly. In these cases, you need to ask yourself, "Which do I value more:

my pride or this relationship?" Remember, when you take responsibility for your bad behavior, you're showing your commitment to reason and to the relationship.

Lastly, put a lot of effort into finding and building relationships with people who are just as committed as you are to improving quality of mind. You'll benefit by enjoying their company, but also from almost a kind of osmosis that can supercharge your progress toward a better quality of mind.

Relationship Knowledge Recommendation

In any relationship (intimate, familial, platonic, professional) the terms that must be defined are the ones connected to expectations and roles. Although at first blush it may seem to diminish the nature of the relationship, writing these down in clear and concise terms proves quite beneficial. It's of tremendous value to be certain that both or all parties agree with the terms of the relationship, so as to avoid conflict. It also helps you adjust as the relationship evolves. Imagine the futility of two people attempting to correct a relationship that they have never properly defined.

Author and facilitator Alexandra Elle says, "Compromise, communication, and consistency are needed in all relationships, not just romantic ones."

Recommended Reading

The Guide to Strong Relationship Boundaries by Mark Manson, *https://markmanson.net/boundaries*

Relationship Understanding Recommendation

When examining potential problems and their possible solutions, make every effort to take emotion out of the equation. Instead, apply the terms by which the relationship was defined. It's fair to say that relationships are the most challenging area to properly apply logic and reason, while minimizing the distracting influence of emotions. Acknowledging this will allow you to be kinder to yourself and the other party. However, you shouldn't be kind to the point of surrendering your self-respect or commitment to reason.

As novelist Khaled Hosseini says, "Don't be afraid to tell the truth. It's better to hurt someone by truth than to make them happy by lies."

Recommended Reading

The Laws of Human Nature by Robert Greene

Relationship Wisdom Recommendation

Decisions to pursue, end, begin, or alter terms of a relationship will stand firmer when they are made based upon agreed terms and thoughtful evaluation. Being up front about the knowledge and understanding of the relationship allows all parties involved to maintain healthy levels of respect and dignity.

According to Dr. Asa Don Brown, "The key to healthy communication is having a willingness to lay aside our defensive tendencies and accept responsibility for our part of the relationship."

Recommended Reading

The Mindfulness Toolbox for Relationships: 50 Practical Tips, Tools & Handouts for Building Compassionate Connections by Donald Altman MA, LPC

Chapter 9

HEALTHCARE

A judge sits silently over a trial, never giving the jury instructions or ruling on the admissibility of evidence.

The lawyers sit quietly at their respective tables, never rising to ask questions of witnesses. They make no opening or closing statements to the jury.

One person after another enters the witness box, gives evidence, and then leaves. There's no way for an independent observer to determine what's relevant and what's not.

At the end, the jury renders what they refer to as an "evidence-based" verdict, but there's no way for an onlooker to determine the truth of the verdict.

Is this the plot to a sequel of Franz Kafka's novel *The Trial*? No. But this surreal scenario is the perfect analogy for how "evidence-based healthcare" works in practice.

Evidence-based healthcare is pervasive now, and despite how it sounds, it's an illogical way to approach our health. I'm not against evidence, of course. Evidence is fantastic, and we'd be foolish to ignore it.

The problem is that it's only the first step of the trivium. We should be gathering knowledge, defining terms, and weighing facts to see if they accurately reflect reality. But those should be the premises, not the conclusions.

With evidence-based healthcare, we're supposed to "listen to the evidence." The step that's missing is applying logic to the evidence. The assumption seems to be that the right actions will magically emerge by blindly imitating the results of a study.

That's exactly like the fictional trial at the beginning of this chapter. We aren't given enough context to determine what evidence is relevant, the judge has given no instructions to the jury to help in understanding, and the lawyers aren't cross-examining the evidence.

Even many in the field recognize the problems with evidence-based care, but the entire industry can't seem to break free from its grip. No one wants to be called out as anti evidence.

One common criticism, even from within the medical community that practices it, is that treatments often defy common sense, and lead to interventions that are illogical when seen in the context of a specific patient. The rationale can become, "This is what insurance will cover, this is what will be done."

Another big issue is with the word itself. People hear evidence and think they shouldn't question it in medical matters. Why? Who says? We question the evidence all the time in other areas of life, including scientific research, news editorials, and forensics.

Perhaps people think that this must be different because it's science. This reveals a fundamental misunderstanding of science as a category. As we discussed in a previous chapter, science is a body of knowledge that keeps changing. You sometimes hear, "You can't argue with science." That's wrong. That's what scientists do all the time, with each other, with data, with hypotheses. What you can't argue with is truth: accurate premises (grammar/input/knowledge) filtered through the laws of reason (logic/processing/understanding), from which emerges the truth, which should then be acted on (rhetoric/output/wisdom).

The idea of science is that the quantity and quality should always be improving. As we acquire more knowledge/evidence, we verify it, and we add to it, which increases the quantity. We look for contradictions, errors in reason, and logical inconsistencies, and then revise our output, which increases the quality.

There's another criticism of evidence-based care that is well documented: most intervention studies are industry sponsored.

The typical study is done in a university setting. The universities get large sums of grant money to fund studies from biomedical corporations, which are companies that sell medical intervention equipment and pharmaceuticals.

Is this like the old days when the tobacco industry would sponsor studies that purported to show that tobacco was actually good for you? No, it's not that blatant. But because it's less obvious, and because people can't see through it as easily, in some ways it's worse and more insidious.

It's all under the guise of care, but these large, hospital-owned practices have shareholders. Those donating money for studies at universities also have shareholders, who expect a return on investment. The profit motivation is often cloaked, but it's there.

This is why the term evidence-based sounds so good but is so misleading. Researchers can select the evidence that matches their expectations and self-interest (oftentimes without even realizing it themselves) and call it unassailable evidence. But they're not always unbiased. The context is important.

Individuals, institutions, and entire industries aren't interested in letting competing paradigms and their associated products and services take root and harm their business model. That would impact them financially and lower their cultural prestige.

This means the overall evidence has a good chance of being incomplete or biased or both. It shouldn't surprise us that with special interests in play, patients may be given less effective, harmful, or more expensive treatments. All that completely contradicts the supposed major reason for evidence-based care.

Evidence-based care is rarely defined precisely, but it typically also involves "patient preference" as one of its criteria for recommending treatment. This is another one of those things that sounds good but shows the internal contradictions of evidence-based care.

Patients, of course, should have the freedom to choose their care or even refuse any care. But that's different from saying that their choice should impact the recommendation, particularly in a system of healthcare that claims to be evidence-based.

If you're going for major heart surgery, your preferences should not matter at all to the cardiac surgeon. That should have no effect on the recommended course of treatment. This isn't a haircut with you deciding what style you like.

Understanding Evidence

Our goal should be to aim for logic-based care, which would mean we'd stop blindly following data and instead use logic to sift the evidence to come up with better treatment recommendations.

Let's look a little deeper at how evidence is used in the current paradigm. The highest-quality evidence is supposed to be systematic, peer-reviewed study, or a meta-analysis of randomized control trials, from which we derive evidence-based practice guidelines. These are considered the strongest levels of evidence on which to guide care decisions.

Let's break this down, and look at peer reviews, which tend toward herd thinking, based on academic peer pressure.

Here's an analogy. Let's say we're studying ancient Egypt. If we wanted a complete picture, we'd want to get perspectives of archeologists, historians, geologists, engineers—anybody that could add a helpful perspective. A true comprehensive look and peer review of research on ancient Egypt would need to have multiple disciplines involved and integrate them into a real review of the research.

In healthcare, by contrast, peer reviews typically all come from within the same discipline. They have the same education, the same outlook on what medicine is for, and have similar degrees. A true review would widen from this narrow viewpoint.

But even if peer-reviewed doesn't mean much, surely randomized control trials are unassailable. They sound good, and in some cases are valuable data if used logically. But randomized trials can also be deceptive because of how many variables can come into play when it comes to health.

Let's say that we want to do an experiment with plants. We have two identical plants in two identical pots. They're both housed in the same dark room as an environment. One we water, and one we don't. The experiment goes for two weeks, and both plants end up dead. The evidence shows us that water makes no difference to plants.

But maybe we spot a problem with our variables. Now we need four plants. One gets sun and water. One gets sun and no water. One gets no sun but gets water. And one gets no sun and no water. At the end of the experiment, all the plants are again dead. The evidence is that water and sun don't help plants.

Now I need eight plants, because the soil in the previous experiments didn't contain potassium or nitrogen. So I would set up eight different combinations of water/no water, sun/no sun, enriched soil/poor soil. And on it goes.

Let me point out a few things about this example. I intentionally made it extremely simple to show how many variables go into something we know well and isn't too complicated. Now try and control for something unlike plants, which we know need water, sun, and good soil. Randomized control trials by definition need to "control" as many factors as possible. But that can make trials turn out results that seem to produce evidence, but when you look closely, not all variables can be controlled for. And if you control for too many variables, that can also limit the usefulness of the results. There are problems both ways.

Let's have a little fun and bring back Santa Claus again, this time for an evidence-based experiment. You're a child and you put out cookies and milk every Christmas Eve. Year after year, you wake up and the milk glass is empty, and all that is left of the cookies are a few crumbs.

Let's say you began doing this at age three and now you're eight. The results have always been the same. After five years, you have plenty of evidence. The experiment has consistently produced the same result.

Here's something else to consider: this particular experiment couldn't be better peer reviewed. Every year, millions of kids are doing the same experiment and getting the same results. Milk gone. Cookie plate empty. Presents under the tree. Stockings stuffed. That's evidence, and it's confirmed all over the world.

Evidence does not mean proof. That's easy to see in the plant experiment and in the Santa Claus example. But because we've been indoctrinated in the blind faith of evidence-based practice, we overlook the possibility of being misled by evidence. Much of it rests on an appeal to authority instead of logical reasoning.

Don't Call It Healthcare, It's Sick Care

The final nail in the coffin of evidence-based care is that it's not really about healthcare. It's sick care. The fundamental orientation of most healthcare today is an absence of symptoms.

To get to an understanding of the difference between true healthcare versus sick care, we need to use the trivium and start by defining our terms. In this instance, the key is to define what is meant by health.

We've been trained by the medical industry to think that health means being able to say, "I feel good and don't have any pain." The healthcare industry reinforces this by being mostly interested in the absence of disease and/or the absence of symptoms.

However, the World Health Organization and their own medical dictionaries define health in a positive way, as a state of complete physical, mental, and social well-being.

In other words, health is not about absence; it's about optimal function.

When you begin to see that health is about function instead of feeling, you realize that health should not be defined by the absence of symptoms and pain.

If you have an infection, your temperature rises. If you eat bad food, your body's intestines react to expel it. You may vomit to reject a virus. You cough, you sneeze as reactions to things impairing the body's function. None of the above feels good, and they are symptoms, but it's your body functioning properly to remove toxins. It's possible to feel horrible while your body is completely healthy, when you realize health is a properly functioning body.

Here's an opposite example. Let's say someone has aches and pains related to arthritis. They decide to take some morphine or heroin to stop the pain. It works, but are they healthy? We know the answer. Heroin addicts feel good a lot of the time, but I very much doubt you'd call them healthy.

You can see that any definition of health as simply "feeling good" or an absence of symptoms or pain is wrong. It's a poor defining of terms. But this faulty definition is what most if not all of our insurance-approved healthcare is based on.

We've all been trained to go to the doctor when you're sick or have symptoms, and rarely otherwise. The wider context of healthcare based on a more natural definition of health is lost.

A typical visit to a medical doctor goes like this: she examines your symptoms and gives you something to reduce the symptoms. You don't go home healthy. Your body still needs to adapt, heal, or repair the underlying cause.

In some cases, your body must now work harder to support health. For example, your liver and kidneys may need to repair the damage done by the medication you were prescribed. In other words, the sick care paradigm can actually suppress the body's systems that support health. You may feel better, but the care you're receiving is not supporting healthy function.

The Five Signs of Life

How can we adopt a more logical approach to healthcare? If evidence-based medicine and an emphasis on sick care are failing us, what can we do?

We return to definitions. Choosing to prioritize a well-functioning body is a start. But we need to look closer at what we mean by function and health.

At its most basic, we can define health in terms of life and death. Death ends any discussion about health. A doctor never prescribes drugs for a dead person. Health then is by definition about being alive. So next we have to define life.

We can do that by talking about the five signs of life, because they mark the difference between something that lives and something dead.

The Five Signs of Life for Any Organism

- It can adapt.
- It can grow.
- It can reproduce.
- It can assimilate.
- It can eliminate.

Why are these signs of life important? Because a logic-based healthcare would fundamentally orient itself towards supporting these signs of life. The body has the capability to heal itself through its own healthy functioning, and care should support that.

I had a mentor who put it like this: life is the only thing that can heal life. Here's what he meant. Let's say you get a nasty cut on your arm. You could stay at home and maybe put a cold compress on it or something like that. Or you could go to the doctor and have him put iodine on it and wrap it in bandages.

Which method will heal it? Neither. What will heal it is the body healing itself. Using one of the five signs of life, your body will adapt to the situation and create new cells. That's the only way it heals. It wasn't the bandages.

When you have a sore throat, the cells back in your throat get sick and die. They are replaced by new ones. That's when you're healed. That process will take time, which is why you're down and out for a few days.

If you break your arm, a cast can protect your injured bone as it builds back. But it's the body regenerating and building new bone, not the cast. We forget this, and it skews how we view health and healing. Looked at properly, no healthcare professional, be it a doctor, a chiropractor, an acupuncturist, or a nutritionist has ever healed anyone ever. The best of them practice healthcare in such a way as to artfully guide their patients in letting the body heal using the five signs of life.

Notice that we're rooting these ideas in nature instead of culture. Evidence-based medicine is rooted in the wider culture, with its biases and institutional interests. Healing in accordance with natural processes is more logical because the body is a part of nature.

What about Emergency Medicine?

I don't mean to imply that doctors and healthcare professionals never perform interventions that lead to the preservation of life. Some of the true heroes in medicine are emergency room doctors and trauma surgeons. They are faced with situations where the body has fallen below the threshold where it can heal or adapt itself without a radical intervention.

The ability of the body to heal itself is partly time-based. If you leap on a grenade, the amount of damage done is too much in too short a time; you can't survive it. As a thought experiment, what would happen if each little fragment was time delayed and the damage to the body happened over the course of ten years instead of in an instant. Then your body could likely heal itself. But more radical intervention is necessary when something happens to the body that causes too much trauma in too short a time.

These big interventions are important, but it's a misnomer to call it healthcare. It's actually emergency life-saving care. Advancements in life-saving technology are important and we should recognize that, but it should be a small part of caring for humans. We need to focus healthcare on those things that keep the body out of emergency rooms.

You should also note that these interventions are only meant to buy the body time for it to then heal itself. Life is the only thing that can heal life. Of course, there are limits to the ability of the body to heal. If my finger gets cut off, I can't regenerate it. My body may be able to stop the bleeding and heal over, but it will not become 100 percent the same again.

Returning to the signs of life and using logic to think about them, what else does the body need to help support functioning and self-healing? One crucial support is nutrients. Do we have the ones we need and in enough quantities? Nutrients can impact every sign of life, so this should be a focus of healthcare.

What about specific examples that compare a natural approach versus a sick care approach? Let's say your doctor measures your blood pressure and says it's too high. The response in most cases from sick care is to immediately prescribe something. That may or may not be appropriate.

What knowledge can we gather? What is blood pressure? It's the body adjusting to something, increasing the pressure because of a cause. Could the blood pressure be high because our cardiovascular tissue or the blood vessels are too narrowed by fats, toxins, or inflammation? If they are, then, why? Are there sufficient nutrients to repair and build them to be strong enough?

Is it always the right thing to provide medication to alter the functioning of the pump of pressure? Or should we look at the entire system? With the trivium, gather as much knowledge as possible and look for logical contradictions. The sick care model is to intervene fast and to make the symptom go away.

This is a pattern. You have a fever and your body raises the temperature to kill off the microbes. Many people immediately take an anti-inflammatory to lower the fever. The body is trying to raise the temperature to kill off these toxins and heal itself, and the pill is working against it. Now the microbes are free to multiply and make the problem last longer. However, the client feels they are healthier simply because the fever (that was properly performing its function) has been reduced.

What about diseases that don't typically heal without sick care interventions, like cancer? At a certain point, cancers are past the point where the body can heal itself. And you do the treatments, using reason to determine the best ones.

But this also raises the question: are we spending too much researching treating cancer and not enough on how to prevent it? Yes, because the sick care paradigm has us focused on the wrong things.

Sick care should only be about the most extreme cases where intervention is necessary, and the damage or trauma has exceeded the body's ability to adapt. But instead, this whole mindset pervades the healthcare field. Go to the doctor, even without immediate symptoms, and if you fall outside a certain range, it's "here's a pill." Other options are not discussed, and it is not put in the overall context of what life is, and the five signs of life that define a healthy, functioning body.

Doctors of Health vs. Healthcare Practitioners

Recently I had a friend who had been dealing with long-time chronic health issues. After being frustrated that he wasn't getting better using conventional advice, he experimented with ways to support his body's natural function in place of typical pharmaceutical interventions.

He felt great and returned to his doctor. The doctor seemed a little unsure of how to respond to a healthy patient. My friend described him as perplexed. ("Why are you here? What is your chief complaint?")

He informed the doctor that his health and well-being had greatly improved, and asked for advice on keeping it going. The doctor was flummoxed, but eventually recommended a website with government-recommended dietary guidelines. When my friend read the website content, the recommendations were for him to return to eating the very things he had given up to get healthier.

What happened here? My friend and the doctor were speaking two different languages from two different paradigms. The doctor was simply following evidence-based protocols and then referred the patient to a government website filled with industry-sponsored information. Most doctors of medicine today are trapped in a culture of sick care. The logical thing to do is to find doctors of health who can help guide the body's natural processes for healing.

It's hard to find a true healthcare practitioner who puts things in the context of reason and logic. Someone willing to analyze what physical nutrients you need, or get a blood test to check for toxins in the blood. Does something need to be eliminated? How is the nervous system functioning chemically?

One natural thing to do is visit a chiropractor to make sure that there's nothing mechanically interfering with your nervous system. In my opinion, chiropractic care is one of the most logic-based healthcare paradigms in the world.

When you get down to the heart of the matter, the nervous system controls and regulates every single function of your body. Everything you experience—what you eat, taste, smell, touch, and hear—is regulated and organized through it. There are sensory and motor nerves that detect what is going on internally, like glucose levels, blood pressure, hormone levels, temperature, etc. The nervous system detects that and then responds based on what it finds.

With the nervous system being central to every single function in your body, the logical thing to do is find ways to optimize, protect, and nourish it. Make sure the nervous system has all the nutrients it needs. A good chiropractor uses these premises:

- Health is the proper control and regulation of body function.
- The nervous system controls and regulates all functions.
- The spine protects the integrity of the central nervous system.
- If the integrity of the spine is compromised, the integrity of the nervous system is compromised.
- If the integrity of the nervous system is compromised then health is compromised.

With these premises in mind, the best chance for true health is to maintain the integrity of the spine. The spine protects the nervous system, the nervous system controls function, and proper function is the key to health.

Healthcare Knowledge Recommendation

Make certain that you can discern the difference between nature and culture when it comes to healthcare. Since the body and all its functions operate according to the laws of nature, it's right to conclude that understanding the natural functions of life are the key to better health. Study the five signs of life that distinguish living organisms from lifeless objects: reproduction, growth, assimilation, elimination, and adaptation.

According to the writer and philosopher Voltaire, "The art of medicine consists of amusing the patient while nature cures the disease."

Recommended Reading

Ishmael by Daniel Quinn

Healthcare Understanding Recommendation

Ask yourself if both the premises and conclusions of scientific claims (mainstream or alternative) conform to the laws of nature. If either a premise or the conclusion itself is in contradiction to a natural law, then there is a high probability that any action aligned with that claim will lead to less health rather than greater health.

Voltaire also said, "Doctors are men who prescribe medicines of which they know little, to cure diseases of which they know less, in human beings of whom they know nothing."

Recommended Reading

The MD Emperor Has No Clothes: Everybody Is Sick and I Know Why by Dr. Peter Glidden BS, ND

Healthcare Wisdom Recommendation

Take action with a sincere intent to heal or increase health rather than to merely remove or manage a symptom. If in a life-threatening emergency or when the body is beyond its limits of adaptation, then cultural solutions that are often antithetical to nature may be temporarily appropriate and necessary.

The physician William Osler said, "One of the first duties of the physician is to educate the masses not to take medicine."

Recommended Reading

Confessions of a Medical Heretic by Dr. Robert S. Mendelsohn, MD

Chapter 10

POLITICS

What is it about politics that makes so many of us want to lose our minds?

I believe the answer lies in its ability to hold power over all the other key areas of life. Politics deeply impacts business with laws and regulations. The same with healthcare, whether it be a government-run healthcare system, or one significantly funded by taxes, or one distorted by ever more laws and regulations.

Personal relationships aren't as directly affected, but politics can become contentious enough to split relationships, and government policies and tax credits can influence decisions like getting married and having children.

Healthcare and business mutually influence each other, but it's politics that has the dominant, hierarchical position to other areas of life. The powers are enormous:

- Government can extort money from us with the power of the purse.
- Law enforcement can kick in your door.
- Agencies can set regulations that favor one business or industry over another.

That's just three examples; I'm sure an enumerated list of powers could grow into the thousands. Politics is about how we order our lives together, and it's extremely potent. The passion and frustration elicited by politics is understandable when seen in this light.

The significance of politics is one of the reasons it's so important to employ the trivium when thinking about this subject. The trivium can also help you guard against appeals to emotion and non sequiturs, which are so prominent in politics. The stock-in-trade of politicians is rousing people to a preferred action. The art of politics is to get people stirred up emotionally.

The goal for this chapter is not to tell you what to think or what party to vote for. I won't be wading into specific hot-button issues. I'd rather you learn to think for yourself and come to your own conclusions. What I want to do is point out places where conflicts are rooted in the abuse of terms, and give you some thoughts on how to defend yourself against emotional pleas.

The best place to start is always to define terms. It's part of the first art of the trivium, but it's something we rarely do in politics. Mutually defining terms can significantly reduce conflicts.

For example, if we would properly define terms, we would see that much of the so-called war between liberals and conservatives is illusory. The truth is that nearly everyone is both liberal and conservative (at least in western-style democracies).

We can see this when we look at the word liberal itself, which is derived from the same Latin root as liberty. Liberal means of, or pertaining to, freedom. For those people who are genuinely liberal, and not merely labeled as liberals, freedom is the core political value. That's also true for those traditionally labeled as conservatives.

Unfortunately, the word liberal has now become identified too often with one political party in the United States. Ironically, it's the party that advocates for less liberty and more regulations, including more restrictions on free speech. This moving away from the true definition of liberal has dire consequences.

In fact, freedom is the exact opposite of what they want. Freedom of thought intimidates them, and they want stiff penalties (social and often governmental) for anyone who expresses what they deem to be an incorrect opinion. This is not liberal; it's authoritarian.

So the opposite of a true liberal is not a conservative; it's anyone who is anti freedom.

What's the opposite of a conservative? Anyone who wants to employ radical solutions from either the right or left of the political spectrum. Conservative means conserving the good. Anyone who proposes a radical divergence from that, whether on the right or left, is anticonservative.

The truth is most people are conservative; it's just human nature to be skeptical of radical change or extremism. That does not mean they aren't also liberals (in the classical sense of the word). The best way to put it is that a conservative is a liberal who is particularly focused on preserving what is good and has worked in the past. They believe in freedom, and are not against change, but are wary of radical or extreme "solutions" that cut hard against the grain of what's already proven to work.

The conventional media narrative is that traditional liberals and traditional conservatives are diametrically opposed and are always antagonistic to each other on every issue. It inflates and exaggerates conflict.

This narrative is illogical, and I myself am proof of it (as many people are). For instance, I hold views that would in some cases be considered quite conservative under conventional definitions of the term. I also hold positions on some issues that would be considered very liberal under media narratives. But according to the media model, people are either liberal or conservative, with these categories growing ever more rigid. That doesn't reflect the reality of many people, including myself. The definitions being pushed upon us are simply wrong.

The truth is that Legacy Media is sloppy with definitions, and simplistic with insisting everyone fits neatly into one category or the other. In other words, the knowledge they feed us is not an accurate representation of reality.

Guess which groups benefit the most from this often illusory conflict? Politicians, and the political class that feeds off them, which includes Legacy Media. It also includes the professional activists who appear on media programs constantly. The interest of this class is in stoking the conflicts and blowing them out of proportion.

One of their most effective ploys is promoting a herd mentality. They fan the flames by continuously implying we all should closely identify with a particular group or political ideology. Then they constantly reinforce the message that if you want to remain identified with that group, you'll fall in lockstep on every issue. Otherwise, you are cast out of that identity group.

We can fight this by staying committed to freedom and liberalism. We all should be liberals in the classical sense. We can then debate pursuing those liberal values in a conservative way or a radical way. Conservatism and radical extremism are more about method than ideology. If I'm in pursuit of freedom, I can do that conservatively or I can do it radically.

This all gets lost in nefarious portrayals of conservatives. Even though most traditional conservatives identify strongly with the word liberty, Legacy Media and Hollywood have reinforced again and again the falsehood that conservatives are anti freedom. If you break down their premises and conclusions, what they're really attempting to claim is that freedom can't be pursued in a conservative manner.

Our arguments in politics should be a "family argument" between two views that both love freedom; instead, the message is "pick a side, stick to your side, or you'll be one of *them*."

That's the media's agenda, but it doesn't capture the real conflict in our politics, which is between the extremes on the spectrum. If you talk to people instead of believing that the extremists appearing in the media are representative, you'll discover that the majority of citizens are not extreme. Most people are freedom-loving and don't like extremism or authoritarianism.

Sadly, we're losing touch with this reality. More and more citizens are becoming convinced they need to be more extreme. Emotional manipulations are pushing people to question their commitment to the core value of freedom.

If you're tempted by this yourself, recall your commitment to stay reasonable and remember our shared past. We have a history of liberty, imperfect for sure, but we know how to achieve it and have so far proved we can maintain it. We can have healthy debates about that history and how to best maintain it in the future. However, that becomes impossible if all we do is constantly trigger each other with emotion.

In short, the opposite of "liberal" is authoritarianism, just as the opposite of freedom is slavery. Additionally the opposite of "conservative" is extremism. What we have today is authoritarians posing as "liberals" who incorrectly label conservatives as extremists.

Political Pitfalls

Now that you have a broad overview of the wider-scale manipulation of terms, let's dive into some more specific political maneuverings.

Most politicians stay as abstract with their terms as possible. You'll hear words like "hope." Everyone needs hope and wants a better future, right? How about "progress."

Who's against progress? "Change"? Most people don't like everything, so change will be good. We fill in our preferred interpretations around vague, abstract terms. Notice how politicians are careful not to say what the change will be or what we are "progressing" towards.

The specific premises and logic behind these terms are always left out. Politicians stir our emotions and keep us feeling good, but in the end, it leaves us frustrated when what we thought was promised doesn't materialize.

The only way the trivium works is if we have good input, and that means clearly defined terms. For example, when a politician says, "I want peace," does that mean we should expect to see conflicts resolved through deterrence (more military spending), or by more foreign aid to trouble spots, or by surrendering some of our interests?

We need to define what we mean by peace, then use those definitions to create premises and logical arguments to see if it leads to true peace.

Here's another pitfall to avoid: thinking of a politician as someone you "like" or "don't like." It's common to hear things along the lines of, "I like [insert politician name here]." No, you don't like them or not like them; that's illogical unless you happen to personally know them.

You may like the image a politician projects. You may like the virtues they signal. You may like the emotions they make you feel. But that's all an illusion, like thinking you like an actor. What you really like is the character they project on screen. "Liking" a politician is a celebrity-based approach to politics that is rooted in emotion.

These kinds of category mistakes make us susceptible to being manipulated. Concerning ourselves with whether we like a particular president or candidate distracts us from thinking through their policy proposals and puts us a step closer to being blind followers. Letting emotional attachments to someone you don't know impact your choice for who leads the system you live under is dangerous.

Empty Promises Most of the Time

I have to warn you about the political frustration that awaits you as you get better at spotting vaguely defined words and poor premises. You'll soon find out that it's a very widespread practice, and getting accountable promises from politicians is rare. Slippery words are the preferred currency in this arena.

This is especially a problem because politics is a place where we especially need to work together to tie down how a word is being used. Democracy will not work if we don't have shared meanings. For example, what do you mean by "social safety net," versus how I mean it, versus how a politician might be using it? It creates plenty of opportunities for deception, both intentional and unintentional.

All this is becoming worse. The more we abuse language, and the more we walk away from a commitment to knowledge and understanding, the further we get from the ability to have a reasoned discussion. Instead, it is the loudest, most manipulative voices that control the conversation.

A word becomes useless if the definition is fluid and constantly changing. Politics as we practice it continuously devalues words. If we want to achieve anything, words must have value, and we must share a common meaning.

What Are the Ends of Politics?

If we want to be reasonable citizens, it's important to ask, "For what ends do we want to use politics?"

Politics is ultimately a debate on the distribution of power and the rules for deciding that distribution. For some, politics is nothing more than using influence to get power into the hands of the few. They won't usually say it that bluntly, but that is their purpose. It results in the political systems of monarchy, oligarchy, and totalitarianism.

Others believe that the noblest form of politics would be to distribute power exactly equally among every man, woman, and child. A utopian sounding idea, but impossible to achieve in the context of human nature. Even if it were possible, there's a moral problem, too. This ideology insists on an equality of outcome, regardless of the effort and investment of the individual. It results in the political systems of socialism, communism, and totalitarianism.

Another option is the best form, and the one that best reflects human nature in accord with human freedom: the free market model. It rewards hard work in which those who have the best ideas get elevated. Imperfections in the market are often the result of corruptions, not the market itself. The market under fair conditions raises up those who provide the worthiest solutions. This is how free markets work in democratic political systems.

To recap the three systems:

- **Monarchy/Oligarchy/Totalitarianism**: Total power in the hands of a few.
- **Socialism/Communism/Totalitarianism**: Power supposedly in the hands of everyone equally, but actually most if not all production and distribution is governed by the few.
- **Free Market/Democracy**: Opportunity for power spread equally. Market forces, democratic laws, and individual effort/choices are rewarded and create a fair meritocracy.

Notice that a market works more in accordance with natural forces. You see this in biological life as species evolve complexity with a mechanism similar to market forces. Markets keep us open to appropriate amounts of competition, freedom, and collaboration.

It's true that the third option of free market/democracy does not always work as it should. But much of the blame for that falls to those who reward others who support them with favored status. Power begins accumulating in the hands of the few, creating an unlevel playing field.

Some Final Thoughts on Politics

- Don't judge a politician as "good" or "bad." Stick with judging on principles, policies, and procedures. As soon as we start making them heroes or villains, we're traveling down the path of emotion.

- If you find yourself always siding with the same side of the political spectrum, you're probably not practicing the arts of the trivium. The trivium has helped me change my mind on some political issues by removing emotion and eliminating any need to prop up my identity with groupthink. I've stopped worrying about whether I like a particular politician or party, and find myself free to think outside narrow ideologies.

- Related to this, we've got to stop writing off people and politicians based on one policy position they take. We should be putting each issue under a microscope and analyzing it as reasonably as possible, and sometimes we'll find we disagree on a specific position. This is related to the bloodthirst in social media to track down everything a politician has ever said and done, and flay them for it. All that stuff is an attempt to trigger emotions.

- Look for ways to reduce conflict without sacrificing truth or integrity. Not only does it make politics less frustrating, you'll persuade more people this way.

- The Mainstream Media provides the distribution channel for these emotionally charged messages and the politicians. Big Tech through social media is an accomplice. Consume less of it, or even none at all.

- Don't let emotional authoritarianism—piling on in social media, businesses giving into pressure and firing people for unpopular speech, universities having almost zero diversity of opinion—keep you from seeking and speaking the truth.

Ultimately, you need to discipline yourself to control what you can, and pledge yourself to staying reasonable no matter what others do to elicit emotion. It takes courage to stand up and assert reason when so many are willing to attack you for it.

Oftentimes, things still don't change. Reason doesn't feel like it's close to being restored in politics. It can begin to feel futile. That's when you need to remember that despite all the programming and manipulations, nearly everyone wants freedom.

Your job as an advocate for reason is to convince people that freedom is still viable, but only if we accept the responsibility that comes with it. You can't have freedom without taking responsibility for your own mind.

Politics Knowledge Recommendation

As always, define the terms being used. This is more challenging in politics than any other area, because politicians rely so strongly upon doublespeak, intentional misuse of words, and purposeful misinterpretation of definitions. For example: what does a politician mean when they make claims like "for the greater good," "for the people," "for progress"? Ask yourself if that "progress" or "greater good" has been defined, or did you assume that the politician's agenda and intentions are the same as yours?

As former president Ronald Reagan said, "Politics is supposed to be the second-oldest profession. I have come to realize that it bears a very close resemblance to the first."

Recommended Reading

Doublespeak by William D. Lutz

Politics Understanding Recommendation

Appeal to emotion is heavy-handed in politics, because it's difficult to think critically in an emotionally charged state. Politicians and the legacy institutions that support them play on emotions to stifle quality reasoning, while engendering powerful feelings of resentment/distrust for one party and affection/loyalty for another.

Comedian Groucho Marx quipped, "Politics is the art of looking for trouble, finding it everywhere, diagnosing it incorrectly, and applying the wrong remedies."

Recommended Reading

The Rhetoric of Political Leadership: Logic and Emotion in Public Discourse by Ofer Feldman (Editor)

Politics Wisdom Recommendation

Before communicating with another person or group, be aware of how they are defining their terms. Start all discussions by clarifying commonly held positions. By finding something to agree upon first, influence later will be less difficult. When referring to an idea or proposition avoid using possessive pronouns. For example, instead of referring to something as "my idea" or "your idea," you can better say "another idea" or "an idea." The use of indefinite articles such as "a" and "an" are less personal than "your," "mine," "our," "their," "his," and "her." People are likely to be less defensive when the statements are not personal and less attached to identity.

Writer George Orwell said, "Political language is designed to make lies sound truthful and murder respectable, and to give an appearance of solidity to pure wind."

Recommended Reading

How to Win an Argument: An Ancient Guide to the Art of Persuasion by Marcus Tullius Cicero and James May

Chapter 11

ACHIEVING PREEMINENCE

There's no shortage of people who commit themselves above all to being seen in a positive light. They don't mind artificial poses and they don't much concern themselves with integrity.

To a certain degree, it has always been this way, but social media adds gasoline to the fire. Politicians, social media influencers, and people who have a weak self-image put their best efforts into propping up their reputations on a surface level.

Some of the time, that actually works. However, the truth usually has a way of eventually revealing itself. After a time, the pretending wears thin, and others begin to see that the emperor has no clothes. But even if the reputation holds, what kind of life is that? It's a life of fakery, with no integrity or truth.

You have an opportunity to take a different path. Knowing the trivium hands you the key to developing a life of integrity, responsibility, freedom, and truth. Not a life wasted on figuring out how to present the best reputation to the world.

Here's the best part of choosing the trivium: if you commit to it, eventually, the standing, influence, and impact you want to have in the world will be yours. It won't be on the surface, ready to collapse, leaving you exposed as an inauthentic fraud. Instead it will be deeply authentic because it was earned through a commitment to reason.

I can tell you from my own experience and the experiences of many of the people I coach that practicing these arts will definitely elevate you. As you get better at it, you become naturally uplifted in the eyes of others.

People sense when others are persistently and consistently acting with integrity. It's genuine leadership, not a synthetically propped-up version that requires a constant wasting of energy on reputation building.

The best way I can describe this is that you achieve preeminence. You are distinguished by the quality of your mind, and people recognize it without you having to tell them, or worse by pretending to be someone you are not. They begin to come to you for advice. They want to work together with you in business. You may get invitations to speak. People may ask you to lead in local politics or otherwise help shape your community. All of this because you are truly an individual of authentic value.

What I've noticed in my own life is that people are attracted to me because I've demonstrated value in a way they can understand. It's what drives people to want to work with me, and to use these concepts to improve themselves. I think you'll find similar results if you work at the trivium with both integrity and sincerity.

In this last chapter, I want to leave you with some key themes to remember. It's my hope that this won't just be a book that resonates with you, but then you close it, forget it, and never take action. I genuinely want you to cultivate and nurture the quality of your mind so that your life and the lives of the people around you are lifted to new heights. The trivium is a blueprint for a better life, so let's recall the keys to implementing these arts.

The Three Keys to Maintaining a Commitment to the Trivium

The intellectual effort required to practice the trivium is significant. It also takes courage to stand against the currents of culture. You need three things to maintain your commitment:

- **Understand Its Value:** The trivium is a way to escape from being tossed about from emotion to emotion. You'll instead find firm ground for a life made up of quality decisions. I can't imagine anything more valuable. Reflect on this deeply and you'll realize its value.

- **Desiring Its Benefits:** As the value becomes clear, you'll naturally connect that value to how it benefits you. Things like more business success, stronger relationships, a better understanding of what it means to be healthy, and the ability to defend yourself against harmful political rhetoric. People will recognize you as a person of preeminence and a natural leader.

- **Cultivating and Maintaining a Strong Self-Image:** People with weak self-images struggle to maintain the core values of freedom, responsibility, congruence, and integrity. If you find yourself violating principles you claim to hold, ask yourself why. Maybe you're not valuing yourself enough.

The Role of Emotions

Always remember that emotions are not the enemy of reason. The emotions only become a problem if we put them in charge. Emotions are too variable and multiple to leave in charge of your reactions. Additionally they are in a constant state of change, as they should be; however, this lack of stability makes them a poor tool for reliable decision-making.

That doesn't mean they aren't important. Emotions are feedback about how we're doing, either positive or negative. They also motivate us, fueling our passion to start a business or take better care of our bodies.

The proper thing to do is gather the feedback emotions provide. Then treat that feedback as one piece of the puzzle in responding to any situation. It's the voice of reason that you put in charge of putting together the puzzle; emotions are just some of the puzzle pieces.

Falling Down and Getting Back Up

If you think you're going to be a model of reasoning all the time, let me save you the suspense. You won't.

We're human and we fail. The trivium is the perfect tool for reasonable decisions, but we implement it imperfectly.

We boil over at an intimate partner in a rush of emotion. In a hurry to improve our business, we make a change that costs us money. We allow ourselves to be triggered by something on social media, reacting with our own unhelpful comment in a righteous fury. The list could go on.

When you slip, pause. Take whatever time you need to calm down. Then analyze your mistake using the trivium. And the next time a similar chance arises, do better. Whatever you do, don't give in to futility. Just because we can't be perfect doesn't mean we give up.

The Tools for Living a Worthy Life of Freedom

The trivium is how the mind works naturally. We can find ways to encourage the natural workings of our mind, but any attempt to go against these natural processes is a recipe for failure.

As you become adept with using the trivium, you have a sharpened tool to pick up and use any time. With it, you can independently fix anything on your own and be self-reliant. Without this tool, you'll be stuck calling on other forces to fix things for you. There are large institutions happy to do that for you, but the price is your freedom.

Finally, remember that what's really at stake here is the quality of your life. It works this way:

- You start by improving the quality of your mind…
- Which improves the quality of your decisions…
- And better decisions improve the quality of your life.

Your life can be firmly planted in the soil of truth, reason, and freedom. Commit and reap the benefits.

CONCLUSION

This book has been laser focused on you as an individual. That's the proper emphasis, because it's only through being 100 percent responsible for ourselves as individuals that we achieve quality of mind and a better life.

But, even as free-thinking individuals, we all want to create a better world. A world where reason is restored, conflict is lessened, and freedom can flourish. The surest path to achieving that is the arts of the trivium. The more people that learn about the liberal arts and practice them, the better off we all will be.

Imagine you achieve new levels of intellectual freedom while you live among loved ones (friends, family, neighbors, classmates, coworkers) who are still mentally enslaved. It's great that you are free, but your joy would be tempered knowing those you care about are not. Would you enjoy life if all of your loved ones lived within a physical prison while you roamed free outside? Of course not, and so is it with mental prisons as well. If you're really interested in a better world, then you will start with your own freedom and be the example and preeminent guide to others.

The world won't become better through coercive calls to the "greater good" or other vague abstractions. We can only build a restored world person by person, one individual at a time committing to reason and to respect for themselves and others.

Most people, especially young people, find inspiration in calls to action to build a better world. I share that goal. Unfortunately, many of the calls to action about an improved world are emotion-based pleas to come together in ways that violate individual freedom.

If you're genuinely motivated to shape a new world, you can do no better than to start with yourself. Rid yourself of internal chaos and build inner order by practicing the trivium. With your preeminence, you'll naturally influence others, helping to send ripples of reason out into the world. Spread the arts of the trivium to others; people desperately need to escape manipulation and grow in quality of mind.

A FINAL NOTE TO THE READER

‗‗‗‗‗‗

My admiration for those who recognize and diligently pursue the constant cultivation of their individual reasoning skills cannot be expressed fully enough in the written word. I am well aware that one can lead a horse to water, yet cannot make them drink. I accept that, and bearing that in mind I will continue, as have numerous great minds before me, to lead as many thirsty horses as possible to water that they so desperately need. Whether they drink or not, my work is done.

I dedicated this book to everyone who seeks and speaks the truth, and I recall and emphasize that dedication here in the final paragraph. Standing up for the truth is a noble pursuit and a necessity in our society today. Without the use of reason, we as a species are nothing more than predictable automatons directed by unseen solicitors, who manipulate emotions to benefit a very small group of people. With the use of reason, each can work in freedom and for the mutual benefit of a truly liberated society.

ABOUT THE AUTHOR

———

Dr. Travis Corcoran is a philosopher and liberal arts enthusiast who helps aspiring scholars properly pursue a self-taught education. In addition to owning and operating several healthcare practices in the Netherlands, Dr. Corcoran mentors new graduates on the first three of seven classical liberal arts. Previously, Dr. Corcoran studied nuclear power while serving in the US military and earned his bachelor's degree in philosophy with a minor in biology. He serves on two international boards of directors and, as a college president, donates his time and finances to principled research. Apart from always learning, Dr. Corcoran's favorite hobbies include rock climbing, problem solving and teaching.

CPSIA information can be obtained
at www.ICGtesting.com
Printed in the USA
LVHW091755270222
712102LV00050B/228/J